ALL-IN-ONE INTERMEDIATE + DIGITAL

I0810683

The GRAND Level 4 PIANO Adventures®

by Nancy and Randall Faber

THE BASIC PIANO METHOD

A MUSICAL MIX OF
LESSON
TECHNIQUE
THEORY
PERFORMANCE

This book belongs to: ______________________________

Date: ______________________________

Production Coordinator: Jon Ophoff
Design and Illustrations: Terpstra Design, Wagner Design
Engraving: Dovetree Productions, Inc.

How to Use...

The GRAND Level 4

A **GRAND** adventure awaits students with this inventive, complete Intermediate Course. Repertoire, Technique, and Theory join together for a compelling learning approach.

1 VARIETY OF REPERTOIRE

Enjoy the broad collection of:

- "Grand" jazz standards from The Great American Songbook
- Original keyboard classics
- World-famous orchestral themes
- Faber originals

2 LEVEL 4 TECHNIQUE SECRETS

Acclaimed for developing artistry at the keyboard, the Technique Secrets offer an invaluable foundation for pianism. Technique exercises and etudes support the "secrets."

TECHNIQUE SECRET 1
Alignment, p.12

TECHNIQUE SECRET 2
Drop and Follow-Through, p.13

TECHNIQUE SECRET 3
Weighted Tone and Empty Fingers, p.14

TECHNIQUE SECRET 4
Half Circle/Full Circle, p.15

3 THEORY

Integrated Theory pages address more in-depth harmonic analysis, as well as sightreading, ear-training, improvisation, and composition.

Review: **Tonic** refers to **step 1** of the scale. **Dominant** refers to **step 5** of the scale.

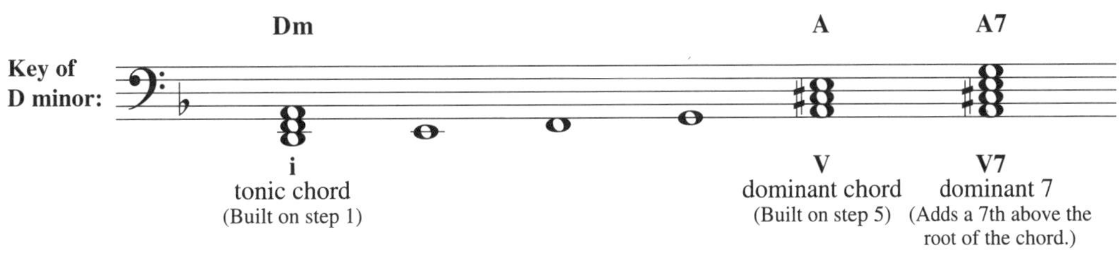

4 ADVENTURE QUOTES

Quotes with each piece encourage students to *"dig deeper"* and *"soar higher."*

5 MODEL PERFORMANCE VIDEOS (MPV)

Each piece and exercise has a QR Code that says LEARNING VIDEO.

LEARNING VIDEO

This links to a video of an artistic performance that features educational text. QR codes for the scales and exercises offer technique variations. These boost skills and ignite keyboard creativity. Intermediate students can *listen*, *watch*, and *create!*

Wishing students and teachers a grand musical adventure!

Nancy Faber   Randall Faber

And now...

The GRAND Level 4 Progress Chart

3B Review: Get Ready for Take-off!

In Level 3B you learned three **16th-note** rhythm patterns.

Rhythm

- Tap (or clap) this rhythm **two times** counting aloud.
  Notice each beat is divided into four equal parts: **1 e + a (1 e and a)**

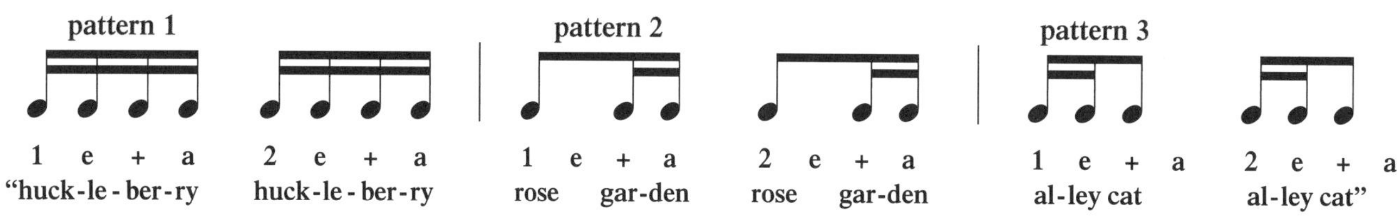

- Write **1 e + a 2 e + a** (etc.) under the rhythm below.
- Then play on a **C chord** at an *andante* (walking speed) tempo. Count aloud.

Ex. 1 e + a 2e+a

Reading

- Name the following intervals: **2nd**, **3rd**, **4th**, **5th**, **6th**, **7th**, and **8ve** (octave).
  Remember to count each line and space, including the *first* and *last* note.

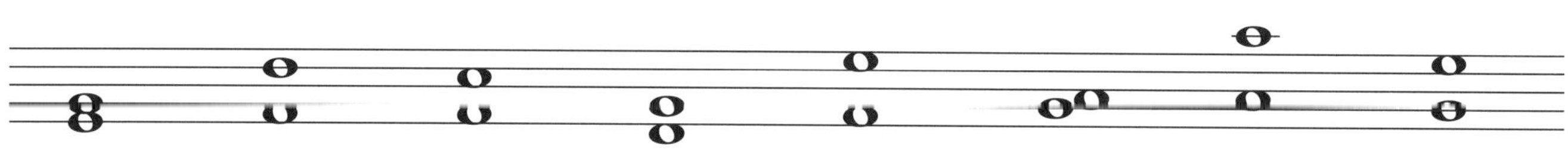

____ ____ ____ ____ ____ ____ ____ ____

- Name these **key signatures**.

____ major ____ major ____ major ____ major

Major and Relative Minor Scales

Every **major key** has a **minor key** that shares the *same* key signature. This minor key is called the **relative minor**.

The relative minor starts on the **6th step** of the major scale.

- Play each scale and listen to the sound.

C major scale

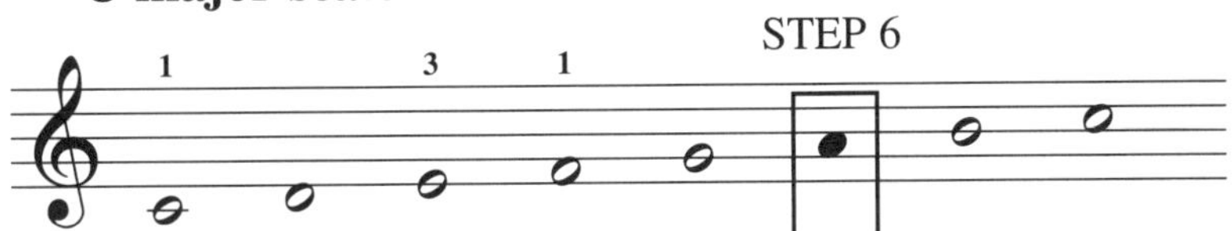

A natural minor scale

- This scale has exactly the **same notes** as the C major scale.

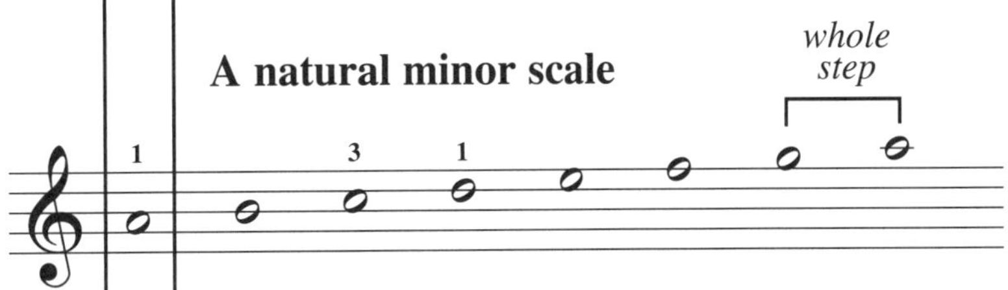

A harmonic minor scale

- The harmonic minor scale raises the **7th tone one half step.**

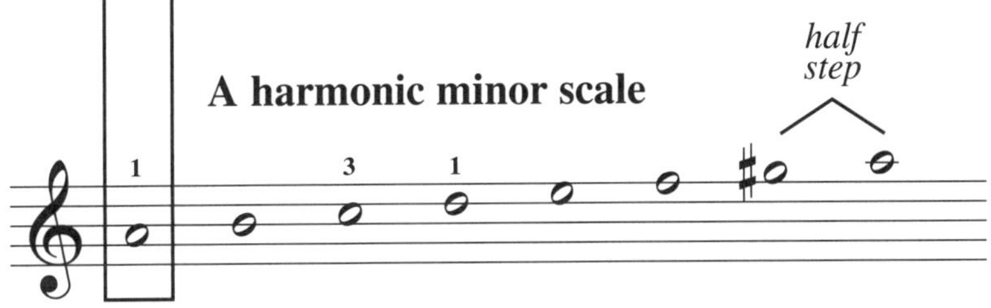

An accidental is needed to raise the **7th step**.
This creates a **half step** between scale steps **7** and **8**.
Remember, this is the *leading tone* to the *tonic*.

Symbols and Terms

- Match the **symbols** to the correct **terms** with a connecting line.

cut time	moving by half steps
chromatic	step 5 of the scale
tonic	𝄵
major 3rd	$\begin{smallmatrix}6\\8\end{smallmatrix}$
dominant	step 7 of the scale
minor 3rd	C - E
leading tone	step 1 of the scale
8th note = 1 beat	C - E♭

Adventure Review Piece: D Major

Review: tenuto or stress mark ♩

This mark means to hold the note its full value.
Hint: Press deeply into the key.

Aurora Borealis*

Key of ___ Major

Andante espressivo

N. Faber

* Aurora Borealis is a vivid, natural light display occuring in the Arctic and Antarctic skies.

DISCOVERY In D Major, the **tonic** is ___ , the **dominant** is ___ , and the **leading tone** is ___ .

The Great American Songbook refers to the significant popular and jazz standards of the 20th century. These enduring tunes were composed for Broadway shows and Hollywood films. In the treasured musical, "Singin' in the Rain," actor Gene Kelly famously dances through puddles in a rainstorm.

LEARNING VIDEO

Singin' in the Rain

Key of ___ Major

- Play the **8th notes** in a long-short **swing rhythm**.

Music by Nacio Herb Brown
Lyrics by Arthur Freed
arranged

Adventure Quote | "Dream. Believe. Do. Repeat." -Anonymous

The teacher should demonstrate each "technique secret."
The **QR Code Videos** are helpful as a reference.

1. The first secret is **Alignment**

Alignment refers to the **balance** of **arm weight** in a straight line through your forearm, hand, and to the knuckle over the fingertip.

- After the grace notes, balance your **arm weight** over each half note.
- Hold and check for a "tall knuckle."

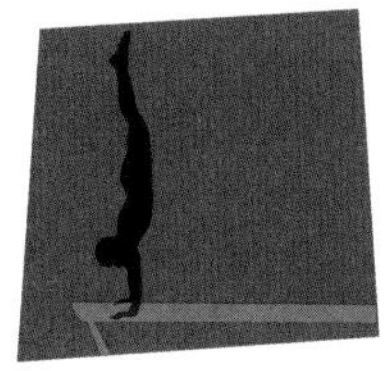

LEARNING VIDEO

SECRET 1

R.H. Balance Beam

Use at p. 16

Moderato

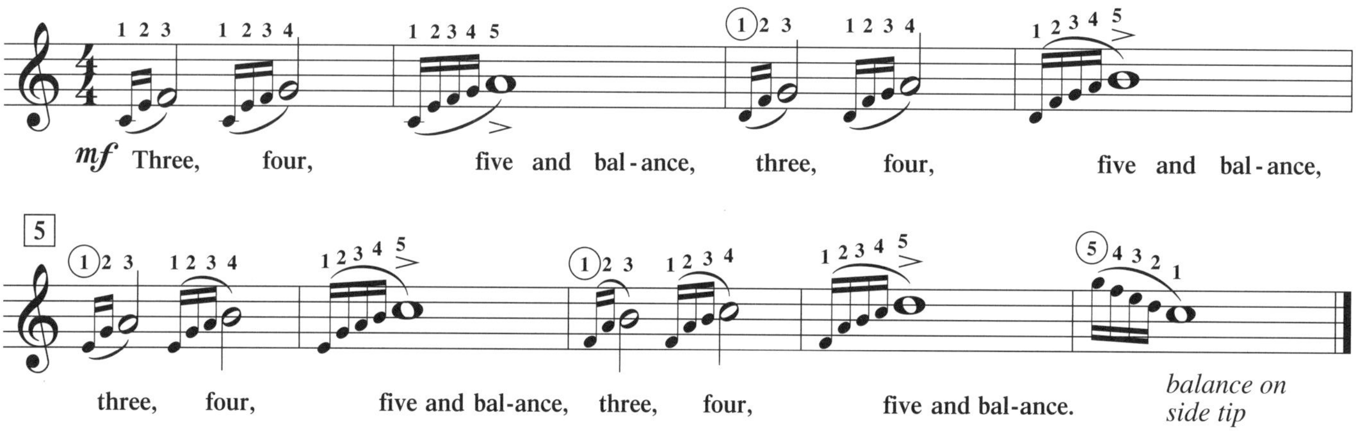

LEARNING VIDEO

L.H. Balance Beam

Use at p. 16

Moderato

2. The second secret is **Drop and Follow-Through**

- Drop with **arm weight** to release a "spark" of energy that carries your fingers through the pattern.

LEARNING VIDEO

SECRET 2

Spark the R.H. Pattern

Use at p. 18

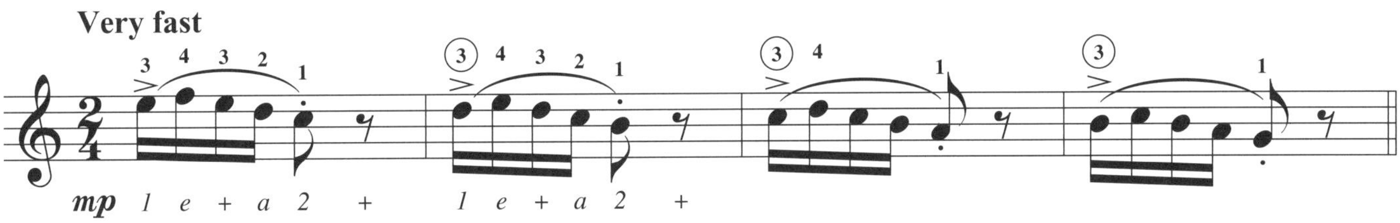

- Continue the **R.H. pattern** on **A**, **G**, **F**, and **E**.

- Now in **3/8** with super fast shifts!

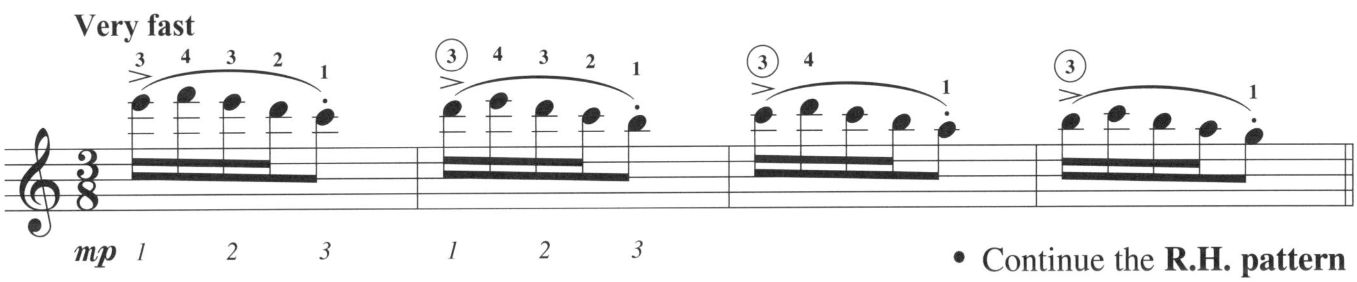

- Continue the **R.H. pattern** on **A**, **G**, **F**, and **E**.

LEARNING VIDEO

Spark the L.H. Pattern

Use at p. 18

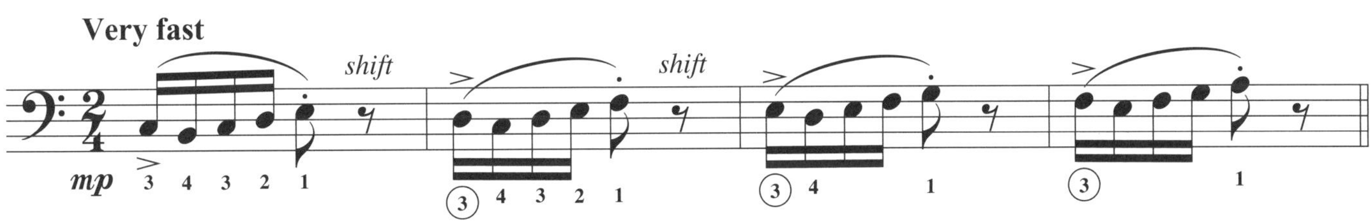

- Continue the **L.H. pattern** on **G**, **A**, **B**, and **C**.

- Now in **3/8**!

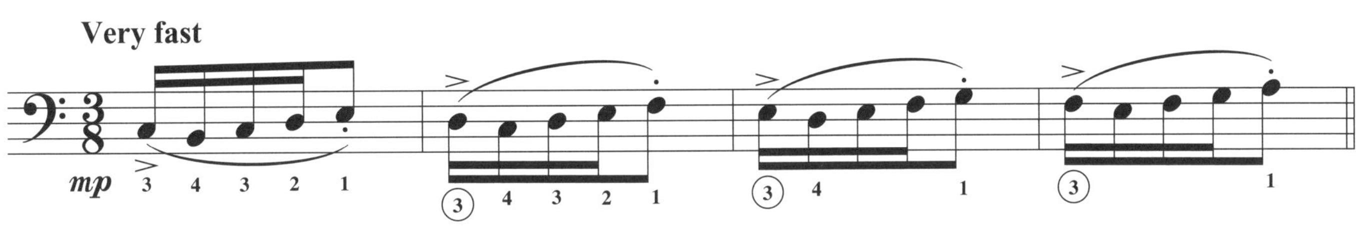

- Continue the **L.H. pattern** on **G**, **A**, **B**, and **C**.

3. The third secret is **Weighted Tone and Empty Fingers**

To produce different "tonal colors," **change** the amount of **arm weight**.
How smoothly can you make the tonal colors change through this passage?

- Begin with "empty fingers"— *unweighted* touch (***pp***).
- Gradually change to a *weighted* tone by transferring arm weight from finger to finger. Reverse going down!
- Notice the brief use of pedal to add luster.

LEARNING VIDEO

SECRET 3

R.H. Tonal Colors

Use at p. 20

Listening for color, smoothly

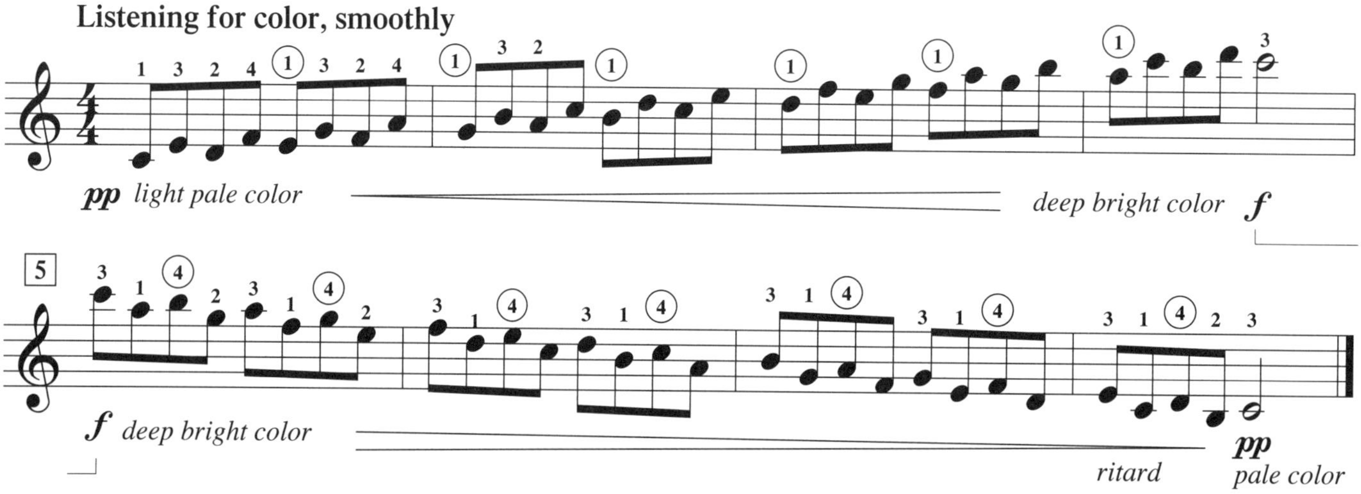

LEARNING VIDEO

L.H. Tonal Colors

Use at p. 20

Listening for color, smoothly

4. The fourth secret is Half Circle/Full Circle

Wrist circles help transfer **arm weight** for proper alignment on each finger. Half-circles can be used for smooth, **wide leaps**, such as this **L.H.** accompaniment.

- Release finger **5** as you pivot on finger **2**.
- Your wrist should rise gracefully to play a *light* thumb.

LEARNING VIDEO

SECRET 4

Pachelbel's Secret (Lead with the Wrist)

Use at p. 24

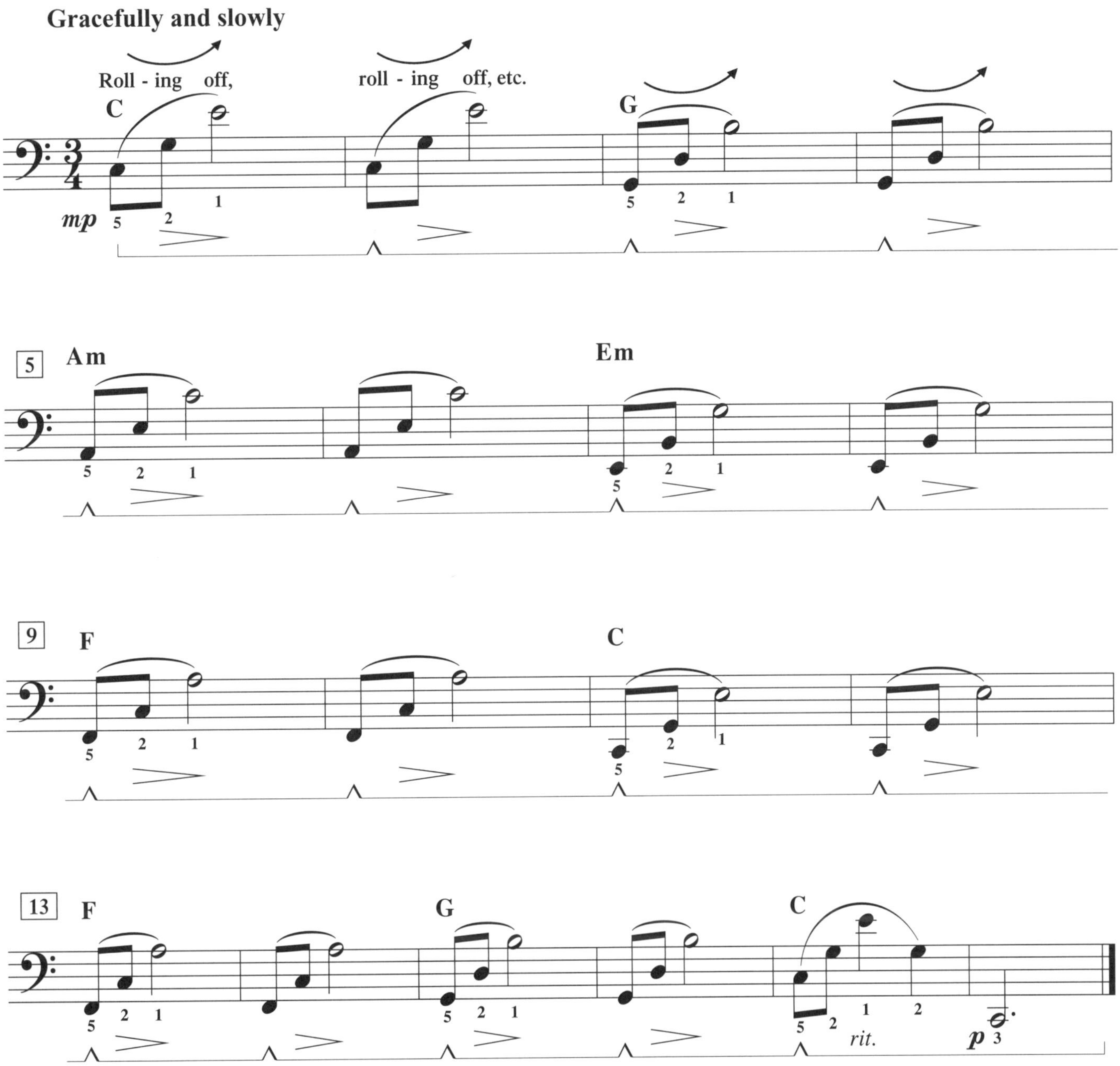

C / Am

2-Octave Scales: C Major and A Minor

Notice the "turn-around" that leads you to the **relative minor**.

TECHNIQUE SECRET 1
Alignment
Warm-up: *Balance Beam*, p. 12

- Memorize each Scale Routine.

R.H. Scale Routine

LEARNING VIDEO

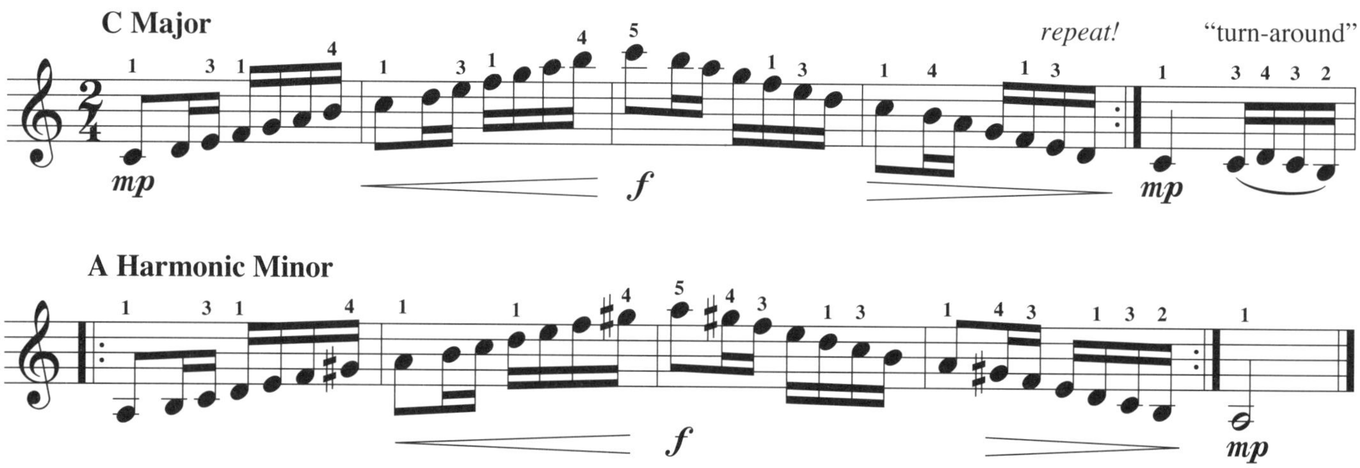

L.H. Scale Routine

LEARNING VIDEO

Optional: ____ ♩ = 72 *Andante* ____ ♩ = 100 *Moderato* ____ ♩ = 112 *Allegro*

Find it Fast!

A quick way to find the relative minor is to count down **three half steps** from the *tonic* of the major key.

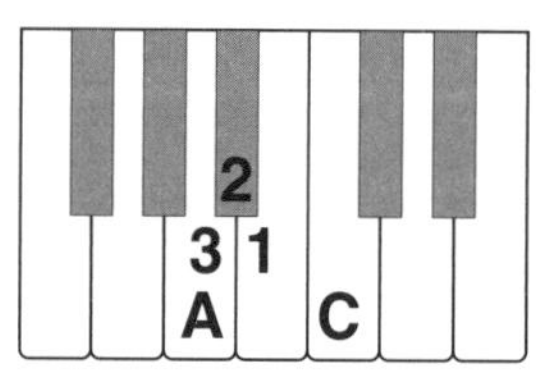

A is the **relative minor** of **C** major.

Major and minor chords have **three positions**:

Root position
The root (chord name) is on the bottom.

1st inversion
The 3rd is on the bottom.

2nd inversion
The 5th is on the bottom.

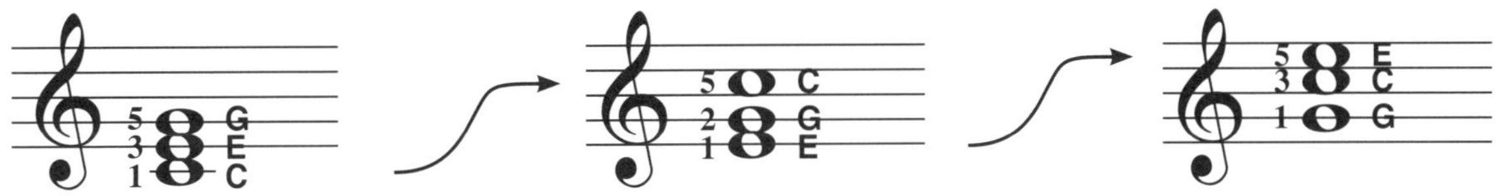

To invert a chord, bring the lowest note up an octave.

LEARNING VIDEO

R.H. Chord Inversions

C Major (C)

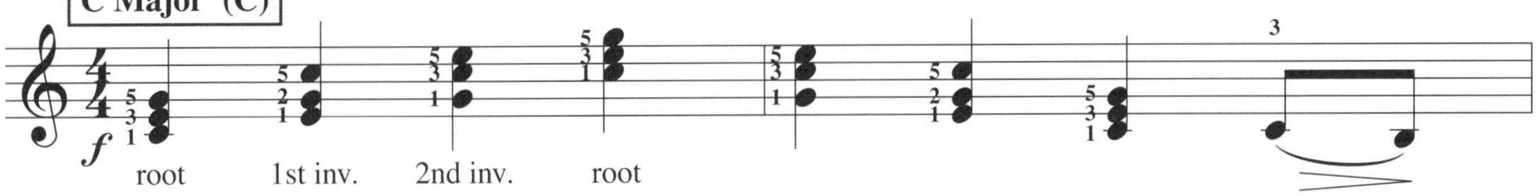

A Minor (Am)

Key of C

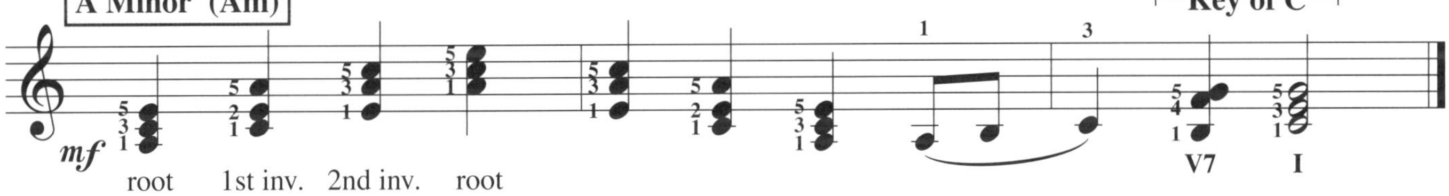

LEARNING VIDEO

L.H. Chord Inversions

C Major (C)

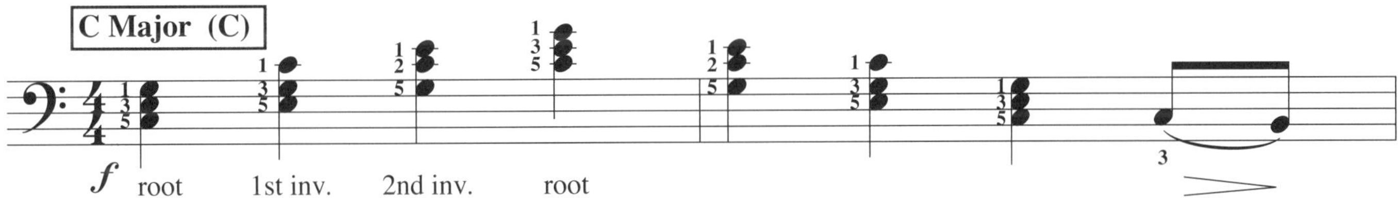

A Minor (Am)

C Major

Key of C: Root Position G7 Chords

LEARNING VIDEO

- Learn this L.H. Etude. Sing or say the words.

L.H. Harmony Etude: C-G7 Chords

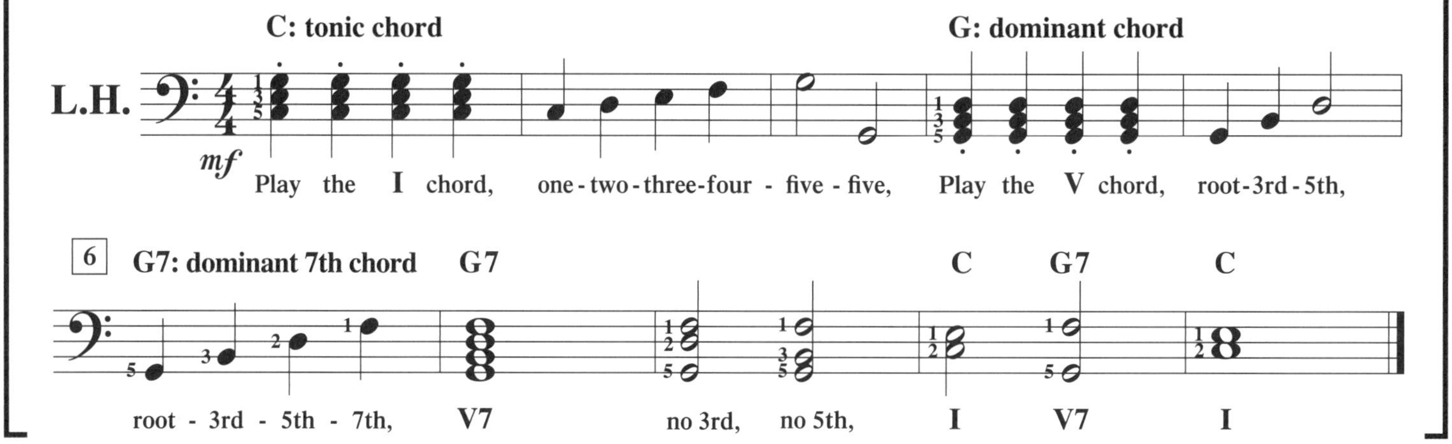

LEARNING VIDEO

TECHNIQUE SECRET 2

Drop and Follow-Through

Warm-up: *Spark the Pattern*, p. 13

Maple Leaf Rag

Scott Joplin
(1868-1917, U.S.A.)
arranged

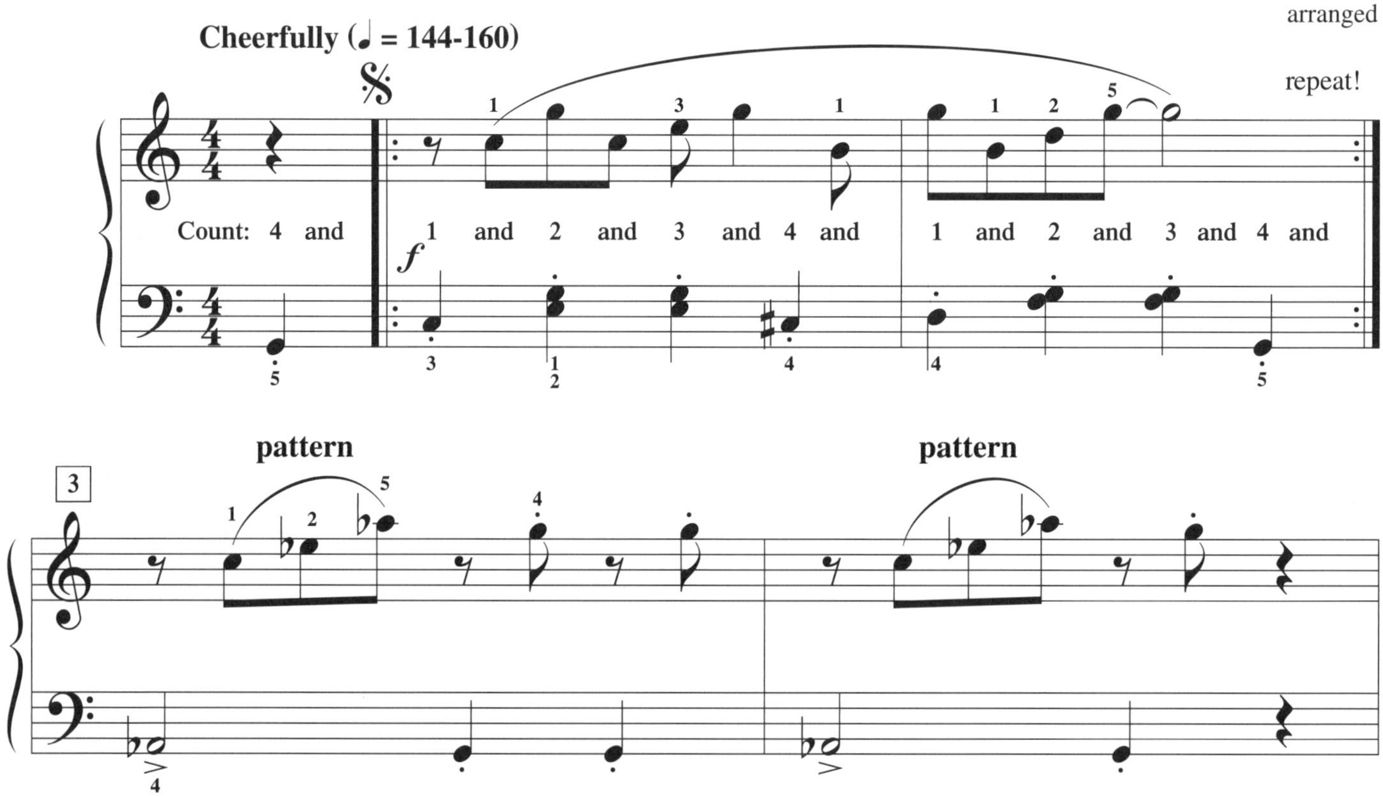

5
T.S. "Drop and Follow-Through"
R.H.
L.H.
cresc.
7
9
G7 C
V7 I
11
Measures 7-10 repeat 1 octave lower!
13
1.
D.S.
2.

TECHNIQUE SECRET 3

Weighted Tone and Empty Fingers

Warm-up *Tonal Colors,* p. 14

LEARNING VIDEO

Distant Bells*

Key of __ Major

J.L. Streabbog
(1835-1886, Belgium)
original form

Andante (♩ = 66-84)

 *Op. 63, No. 6

Adventure Quote | "Music is the space between the notes." -Debussy

DISCOVERY

Write **I** or **V7** in the boxes to show the harmony for the **A** section.

THEORY

Thinking in C Major and A Minor

To find the relative minor key, count down **three half steps** from the *tonic* of the major key.

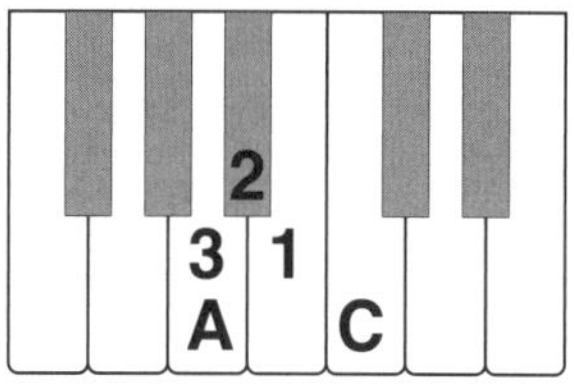

A minor is the relative minor of **C major**.

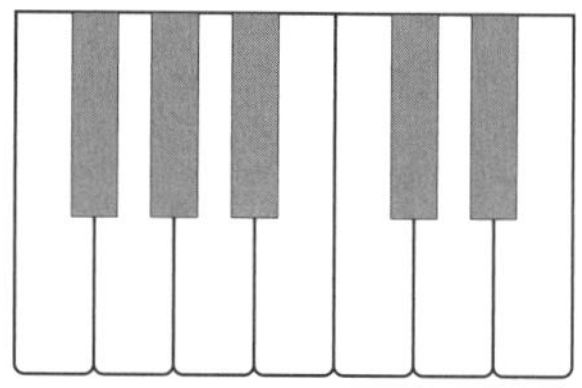

- **Copy** the example to the left.

1. Write a **one-octave C major scale** ascending and descending. Use whole notes.
- Shade each *tonic* note (scale step 1). Label it with **T**. (Hint: There are 3)
- Shade each *dominant* note (scale step 5). Label it **D**. (Hint: There are 2)
- Shade each *leading tone* (scale step 7). Label it **LT**. (Hint: There are 2)

R.H.

L.H.

2. Write a **one-octave A harmonic minor scale** ascending and descending. Use whole notes. Remember the G♯! Then shade and label the *tonic*, *dominant*, and *leading tone*.

R.H.

L.H.

Extra Credit: Your teacher may ask you to write fingering for the scales.

Analyzing I and V7 Chords in Root Position

THEORY

Review: **Tonic** refers to **step 1** of the scale. **Dominant** refers to **step 5** of the scale.

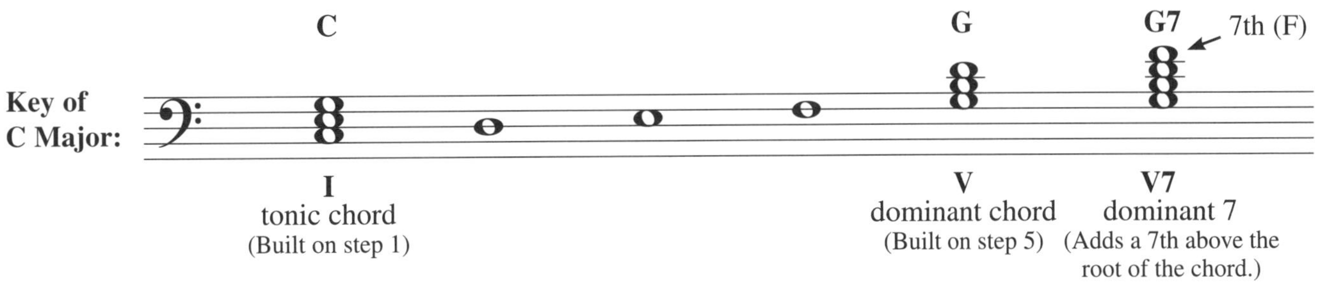

LEARNING VIDEO

- Write **C** or **G7** in the boxes *above* the staff. Write **I** or **V7** in the boxes *below* the staff.
- Circle **no 3rd/5th** where indicated.
- Play the melody and chords hands together.

Horn Call*

Wolfgang Amadeus Mozart
(1756-1791, Austria)
arranged

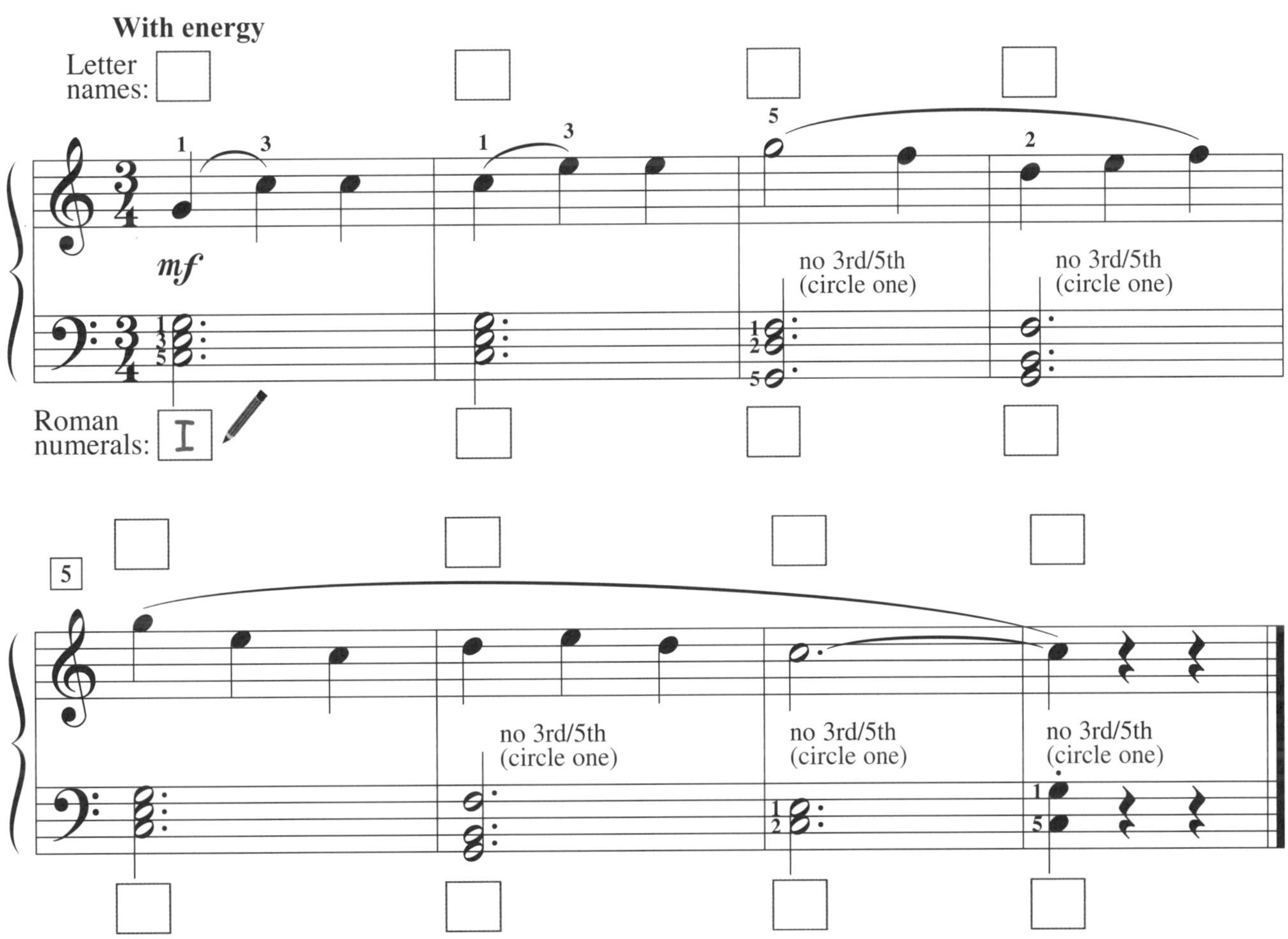

* from *Concerto No. 2 for Horn*

Playing Two-Hand Gestures with Artistry

TECHNIQUE SECRET 4

Half Circle/Full Circle

Warm-up: *Lead with the Wrist*, p. 15

LEARNING VIDEO

Excalibur*

Key of ___ Major/minor

- For each **motive**, use a small "under and over" **R.H.** circular motion. Notice the blue arrows.

N. Faber

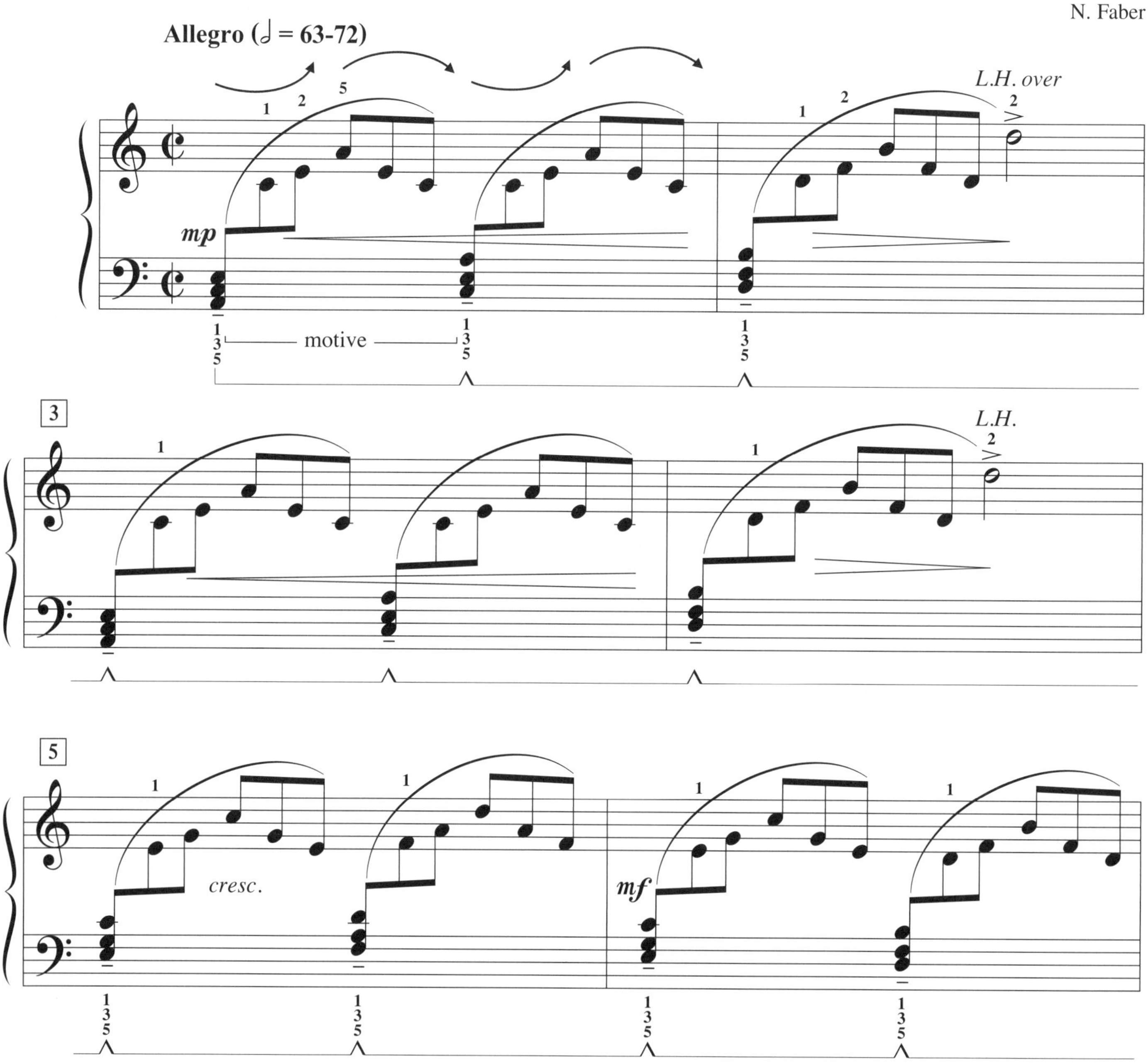

*Excalibur was the magical sword of the legendary King Arthur.

7
1.
L.H. over
2. 3.
To Coda
10
Play with firm fingertips and relaxed wrists.
ff
14
f
p
D.C. al Coda
Coda
f
rit.
R.H.
L.H.
R.H.
8va
ff

TECHNIQUE

Technique Check:

- As you move from finger **5** to finger **3**, balance your **arm weight** in a straight line through your forearm, hand, and to the knuckle over the fingertip.
- Can you play by memory?

LEARNING VIDEO

Make a R.H. Mountain

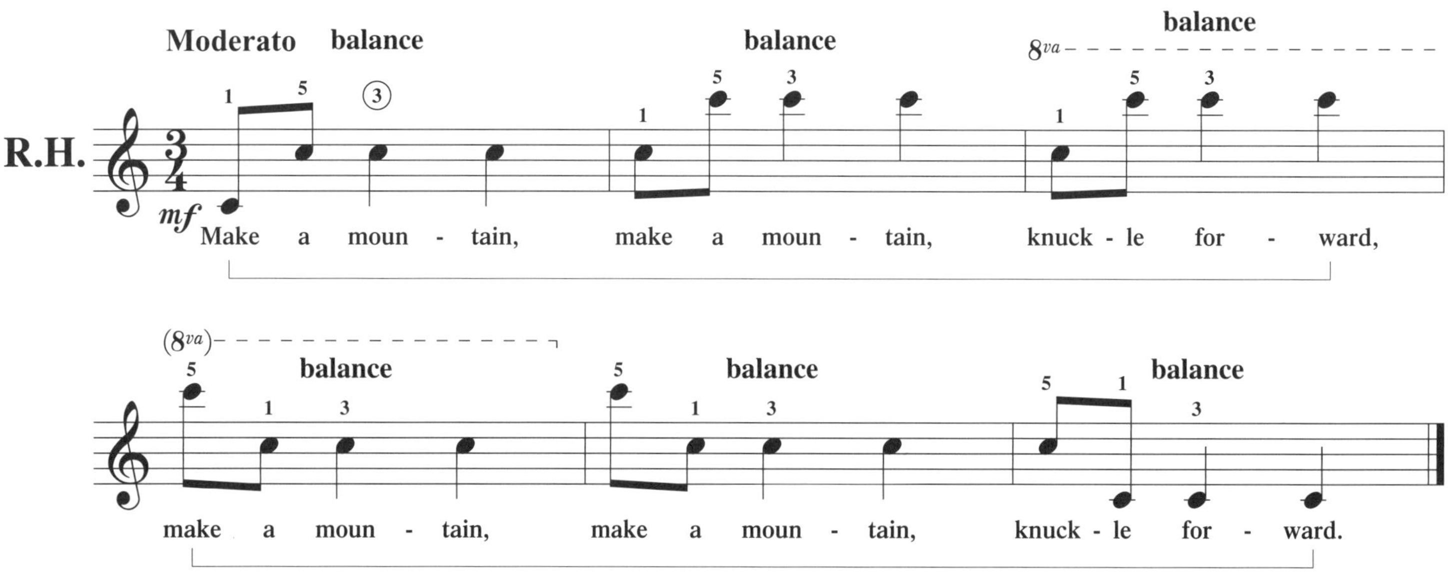

LEARNING VIDEO

Make a L.H. Mountain

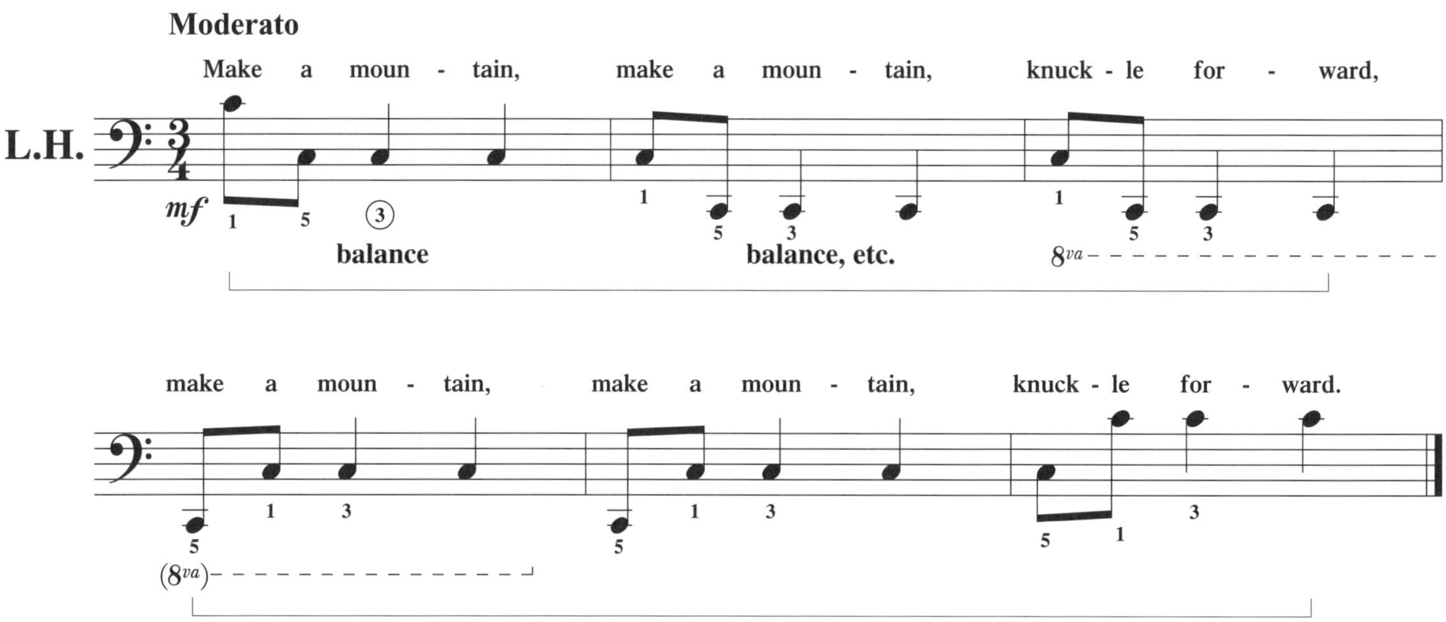

DISCOVERY

Transpose the exercises starting on R.H. and L.H. . You'll be playing the highest and lowest black keys!

Adventure Quote | *"Creativity is contagious." -Albert Einstein*

[When we improvise, we often create sounds using a **specific major** or **minor scale**.]

1. • First, learn this **C major accompaniment**. Play while your teacher *improvises* a melody higher using notes from the **C major scale**.

• Now you **improvise**! (Teacher plays duet.)

C IMPROV
Loons on the Lake

LEARNING VIDEO

2. • Next, learn this **A minor accompaniment**. Play while your teacher *improvises* a melody higher using notes from the **A harmonic minor scale**.

• Now you **improvise**! (Teacher plays duet.)

Am IMPROV
PARTY BEAT

LEARNING VIDEO

Motive and Sequence in $\frac{6}{8}$ Time

Review: A **motive** repeated on another pitch is called a **sequence**.

TECHNIQUE SECRET 2

Drop and Follow-Through

Warm-up: *Spark the Pattern*, p. 13

LEARNING VIDEO

Medieval Fair

Key of ___ Major/minor

9
f
mp
f
13
mp
16
f
D.C. al Coda
mp
Coda
p
cresc.
21
f
rit.
ff

Sonatina Form: First Movement

LEARNING VIDEO

The **musical form** marked in the **blue boxes** shows the structure of the piece.

Sonatina in C

Frank Lynes
(1858-1913, U.S.A)
original form

* Practice the transition over and over for mastery.

Adventure Quote | *"Nothing in this world can take the place of persistence." -Anonymous*

DISCOVERY Label each measure in the **Coda** as a **I** or **V7** chord.

TECHNIQUE

TECHNIQUE SECRET 1
Alignment, p.12

C Scale in Contrary Motion

LEARNING VIDEO

Two Octaves

- What do you notice about the fingering in **contrary motion**?
- Learn and play by memory.

Listening carefully

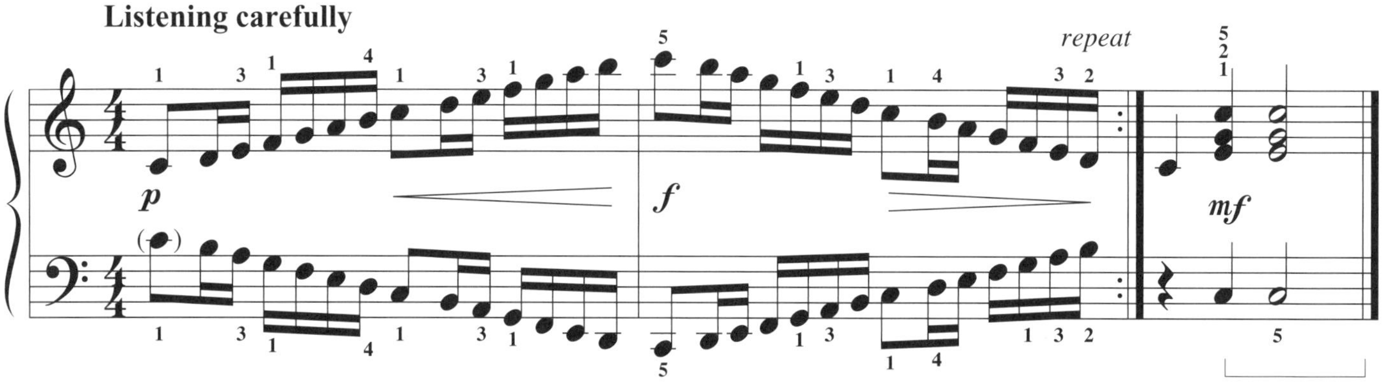

C Scale Toccata

from Op. 101

LEARNING VIDEO

- Here the hands play in **parallel motion**. First practice hands alone.
- Then play **hands together**. Can you play by memory?

Ferdinand Beyer
(1803-1863, Germany)
original form

Steadily

Optional: ____ ♪ = 72 *Andante* ____ ♪ = 104 *Moderato* ____ ♪ = 132 *Allegro*

TECHNIQUE SECRET 1
Alignment, p.12

LEARNING VIDEO

- Practice the **R.H. alone** for fingering and forearm alignment.
- Then practice **H.T.** (hands together) and work up to an *allegro* tempo.

Czerny's Windy Scales

Key of ___ Major

Carl Czerny
(1791-1857, Austria)
original form

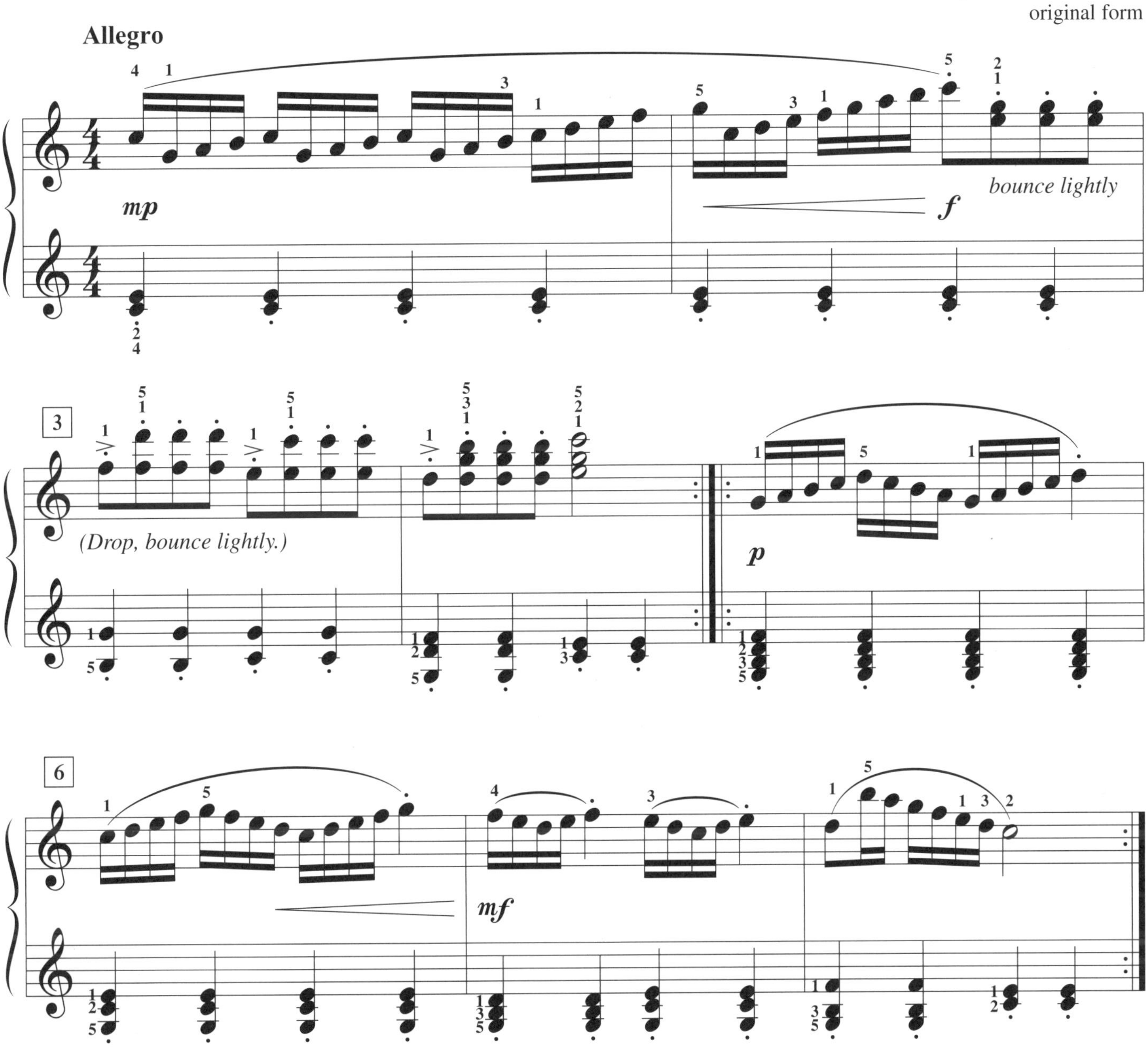

Optional: ____ ♩ = 60 *Andante* ____ ♩ = 80 *Moderato* ____ ♩ = 96 *Allegro*

LEARNING VIDEO

- Learn this L.H. Etude. Sing or say the words. Notice that the **V** and **V7** chords are **major**, even in a **minor key**.

L.H. Harmony Etude: Am-E7 Chords

LEARNING VIDEO

sfz – *sforzando*

A sudden, strong accent on a **single note** or **chord**.

In the Hall of the Mountain King

(from *Peer Gynt Suite*)

Edvard Grieg
(1843-1907, Norway)
arranged

Crisp march tempo (♩ = 100-120)

DISCOVERY

Does this piece begin on the **tonic** or **dominant**? (circle)
Where does the opening melody outline the **relative major chord, C**?

THEORY

- Locate the interval of a **4th** in the inversion.
- The root will always be the *upper* note of the 4th.

root position

This chord is built in 3rds. There is no interval of a 4th.

1st inversion

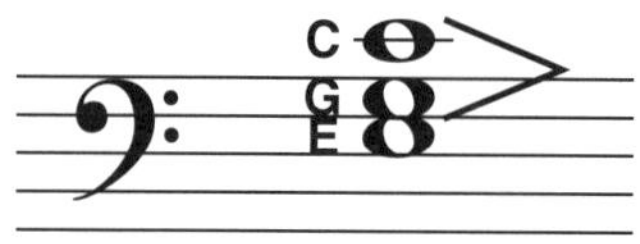

The root is **C**, the *upper* note of the 4th. Notice the interval of a 3rd is at the bottom.

2nd inversion

The root is **C** again, the *upper* note of the 4th. Notice the interval of a 3rd is now at the top.

- Study the top row example.
- Then complete this chart for each keyboard diagram.

Inversions Chord Chart

CHORD	chord root	position	major/minor	on the staff
Ex. 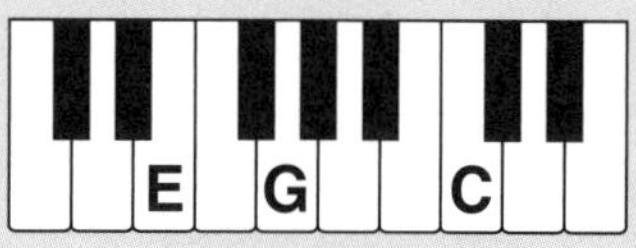	C	root pos. 1st inv. 2nd inv.	major minor	
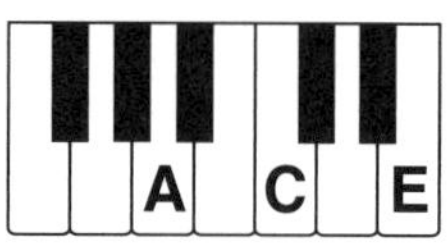		root pos. 1st inv. 2nd inv.	major minor	
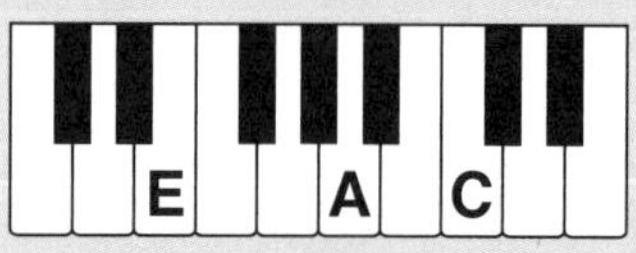		root pos. 1st inv. 2nd inv.	major minor	
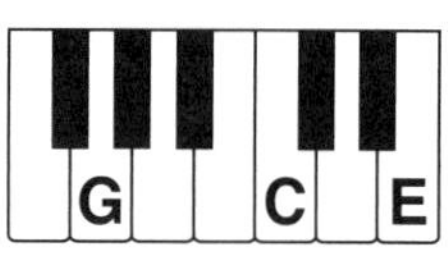		root pos. 1st inv. 2nd inv.	major minor	
		root pos. 1st inv. 2nd inv.	major minor	

THEORY

- Sightread these **L.H.** examples that use **I** and **root position V7 chords**.
  Play each at a moderate tempo.

1.
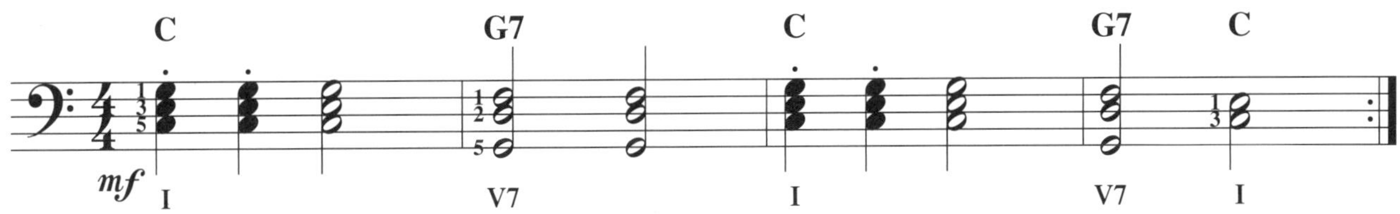

2.

3.
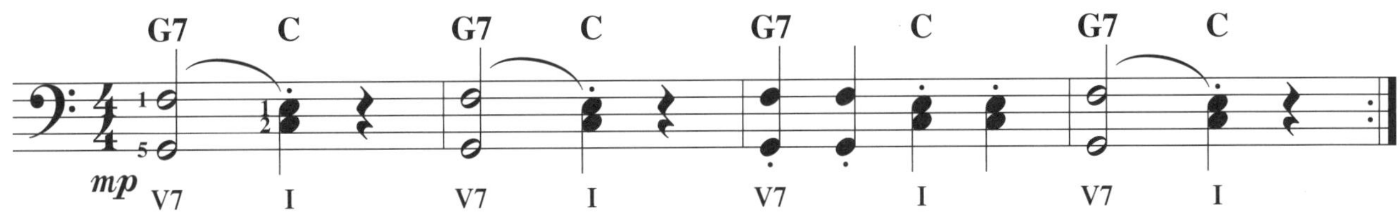

Listen for the Last Chord: I or V7

EAR TRAINING

- Close your eyes and listen carefully. Your teacher will play a musical example.
  Say "**I chord**" or "**V7 chord**" for the final harmony.

For Teacher Use Only: (The examples may be played in any order. Create more examples on your own, if you wish.)

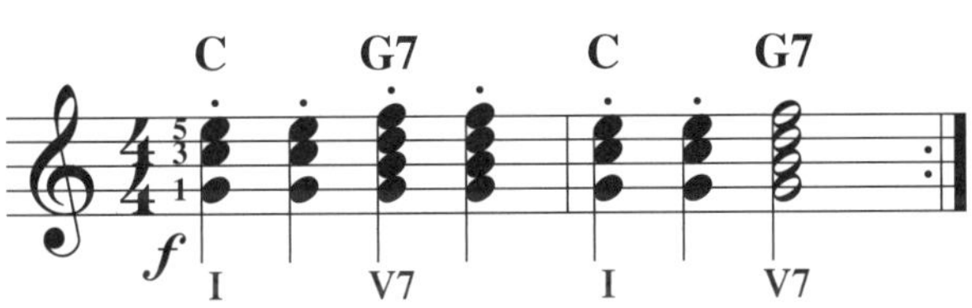

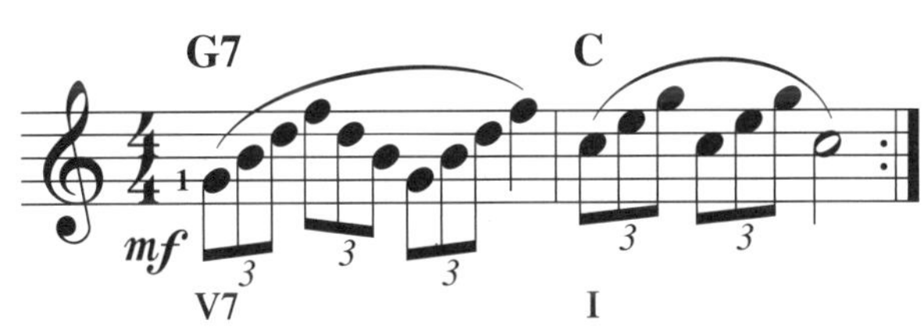

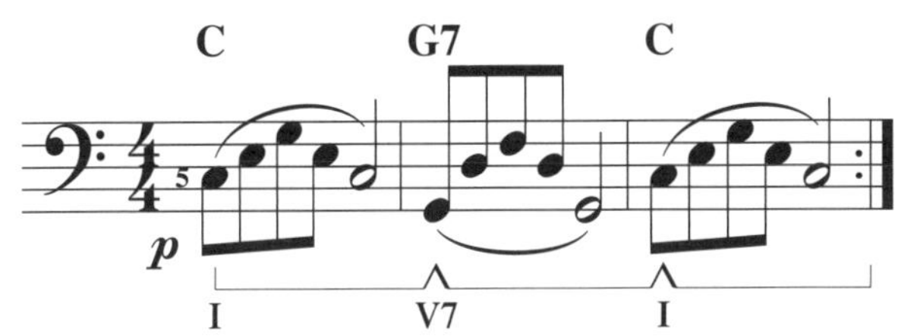

Each unit features a **Challenge Piece**. This is a chance to "spread your wings," enjoy your skills, and acquire more facility and artistry.

Have fun and Take the Challenge!

LEARNING VIDEO

Arabesque*

Key of ___ Major/minor

Johann Friedrich Burgmüller
(1806-1874, Germany)
original form

*Op. 100, No. 2

DISCOVERY

Name the *relative major* key. __________

Can you find a **V7 chord** in the key of the relative major on the first page?

Which note is missing, the 3rd or the 5th? _____

The Dotted-Eighth to Sixteenth Pattern

Count: 1 e and a 1 e and a 1 e and a

1. On the closed keyboard lid, tap your **R.H.** and **L.H. together**, counting aloud.

Count: 1 e and a 2 e and a 3 e and a 4 e and a *(etc.)*

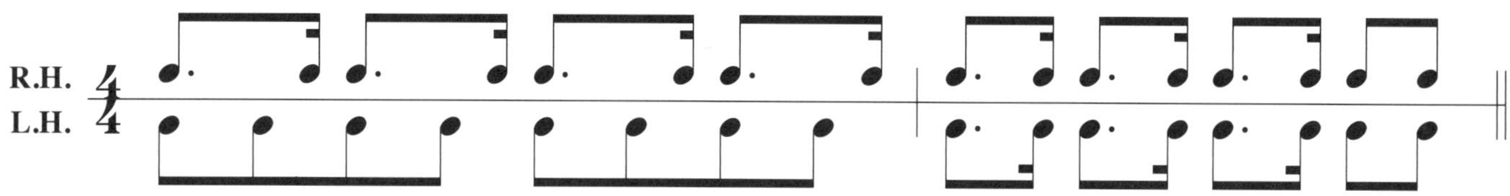

Chopin

Funeral March

LEARNING VIDEO

Key of ___ minor

Frédéric Chopin
(1810-1849, Poland)
from Sonata No. 2

Lento (very slowly)

2.

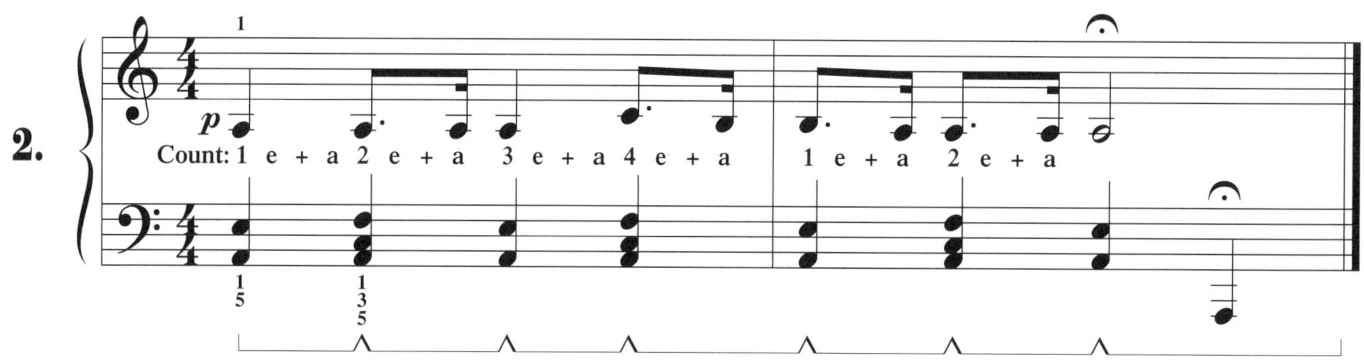

Wagner

Bridal March

LEARNING VIDEO

Key of ___ Major

Richard Wagner
(1813-1883, Germany)
from the opera *Lohengrin*

Andante (walking speed)

3.

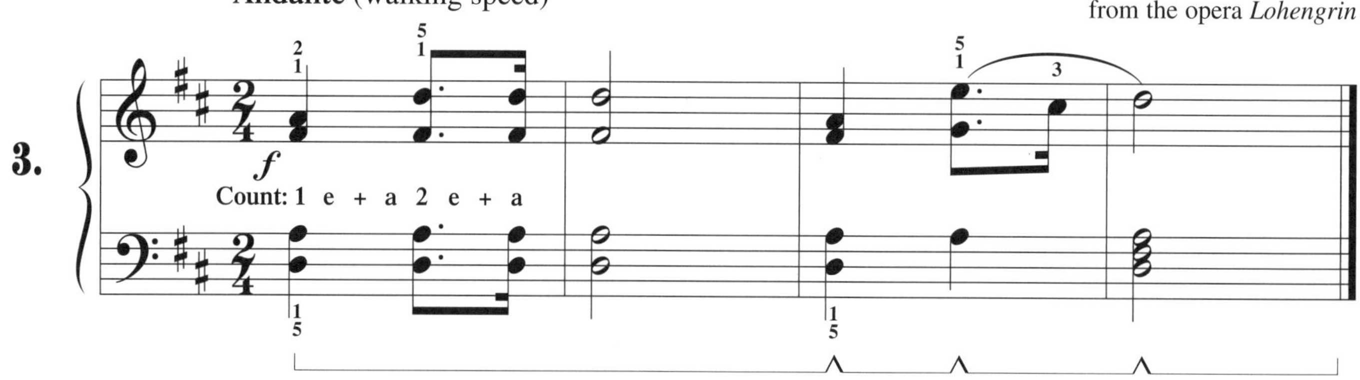

TECHNIQUE SECRET 4
Half Circle/Full Circle, p.15

Arpeggios

LEARNING VIDEO

R.H. Arpeggios with ♪. ♬

March tempo

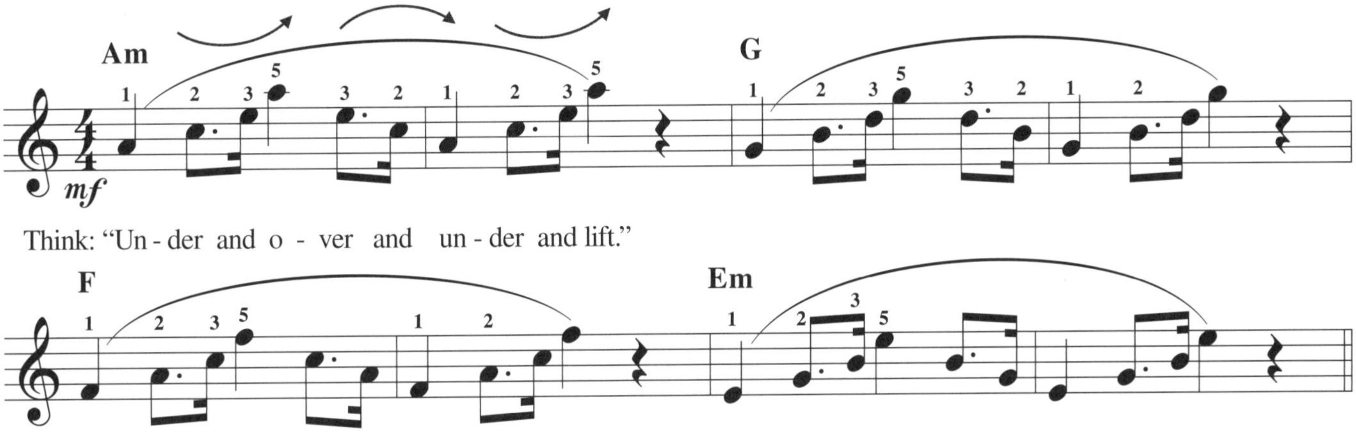

- Continue the white-key arpeggios on **D minor**, then **C major**.

LEARNING VIDEO

L.H. Arpeggios with ♪. ♬

March tempo

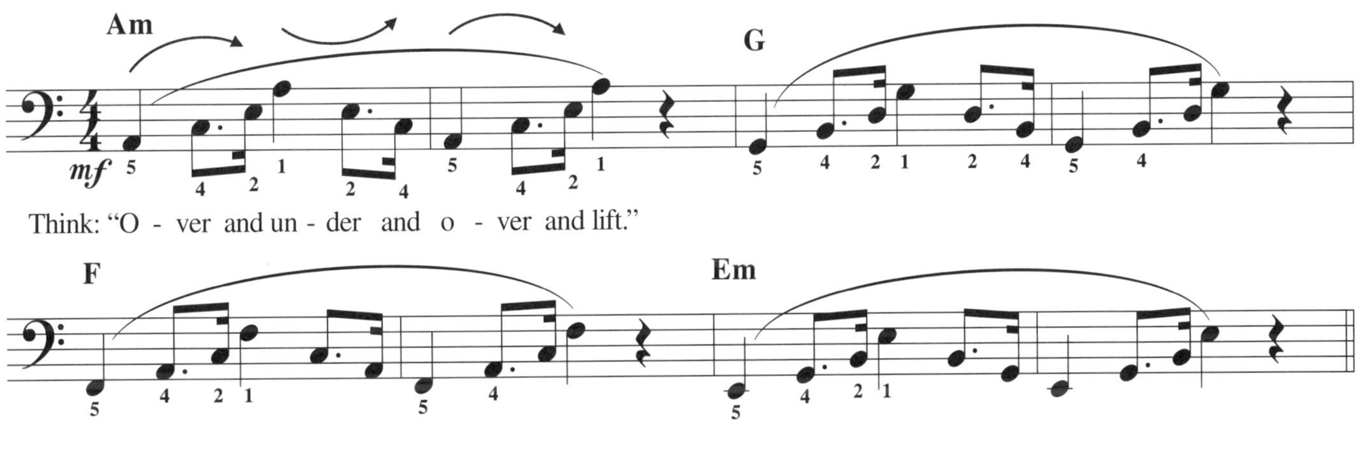

- Continue the white-key arpeggios on **D minor**, then **C major**.

CREATIVE Add a **blocked L.H. chord** on each downbeat to accompany the **R.H. arpeggios**. Now try a **blocked R.H. chord** on each downbeat to accompany the **L.H. arpeggios**.

LEARNING VIDEO

"Bist Du Bei Mir" (pronounced Bist Du By Meer) by **Johann Sebastian Bach** is a famous aria for voice and harpsichord. The translated title means "With You Beside Me." **Anna Magdalena**, Bach's wife, often performed the beautiful piece.

Aria
"Bist Du Bei Mir"

Key of ___ Major

Johann Sebastian Bach
(1685-1750, Germany)
arranged

Adventure Quote | "Soli Deo Gloria." (Glory to God Alone) -J.S. Bach

L.H. Warm-up: Root Position G7 to C Chords

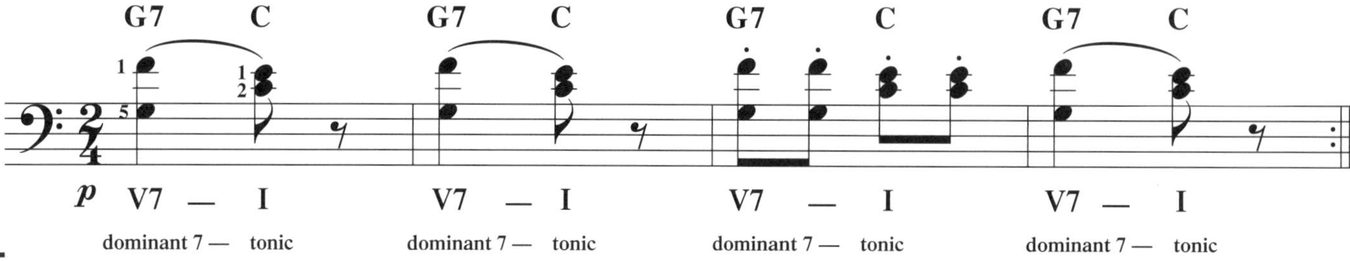

Allegro Grazioso

LEARNING VIDEO

- On what **beat** does this piece begin?

Albert Biehl
(1835-1899, Germany)
original form

Allegro grazioso (gracefully)

DISCOVERY Find an example of these **16th note** rhythm patterns:

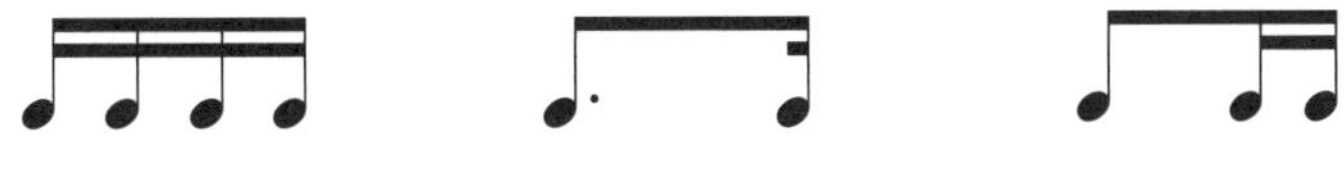

TECHNIQUE

TECHNIQUE SECRET 2
Drop and Follow-Through, p.13

WAMPUS CATS

LEARNING VIDEO

Pep Band 1

Key of ___ Major/minor

• Drop on each **accent** to "spark" the triplet pattern.

Allegro moderato

LEARNING VIDEO

Thunder Hawks

- Similar to *Pep Band 1*, use the **accented note** to "spark" each pattern.
- Play by memory.

Pep Band 2

Key of ___ Major/minor

This **theme** is from one of Beethoven's most famous sonatas. The tempo is marked ***Adagio*** (pronounced ah-DAH-jyoh), meaning slowly.

- Would you play the R.H. triplets with a "**weighted tone**" or "**empty fingers**"?
- Notice the R.H. melody begins at *measure 5*. Let it "sing" with a weighted touch, to contrast the "empty fingers" of the triplets.

Moonlight Sonata

Key of ___ Major/minor

Ludwig van Beethoven
(1770-1827, Germany)
arranged

Adventure Quote | *"I would rather write 10,000 notes than a single letter of the alphabet." –Beethoven*

Jazz musicians often talk about practicing as "woodshedding"—from going out to the "woodshed" to practice in focused solitude. Thomas "Fats" Waller and Harry Brooks were American super talents—jazz pianists, composers, and singers. This song is also part of **The Great American Songbook**. (See p. 10) Have fun "woodshedding" this piece.

LEARNING VIDEO

Ain't Misbehavin'

Music by
Thomas "Fats" Waller
and Harry Brooks
(USA)

Adventure Quote | *"Creativity is just connecting things." –Anonymous*

Count and Hear the ♪. ♬ Pattern

THEORY

- Tap this rhythm with your teacher, counting aloud. Two ways of counting are given.
  Hint: The **16th note** leads into the **dotted eighth-note** that follows it.

a. 1 e + a 2 e + a 1 e + a 2 e + a 1 e + a 2 e + a
b. 1 + a 2 + a 1 + a 2 + a 1 + 2 +

- Turn each pair of **8th notes** into this dotted rhythm: ♪. ♬
  Then tap the rhythm for your teacher, counting aloud.

Ex.

Rhythm and Words

- Copy each rhythm in the box below.
- Draw a line connecting each rhythm to the words that match the sound.

a.

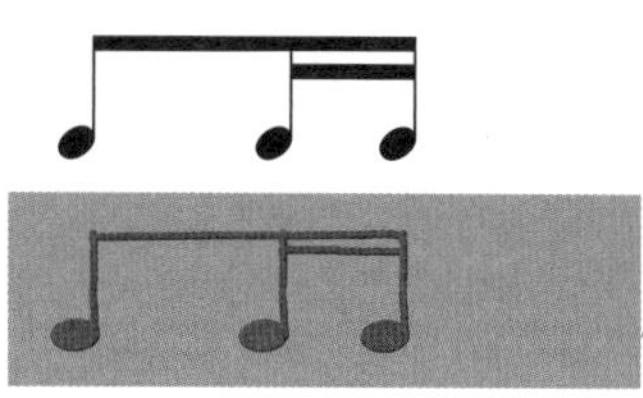

Ex.

b.

c.

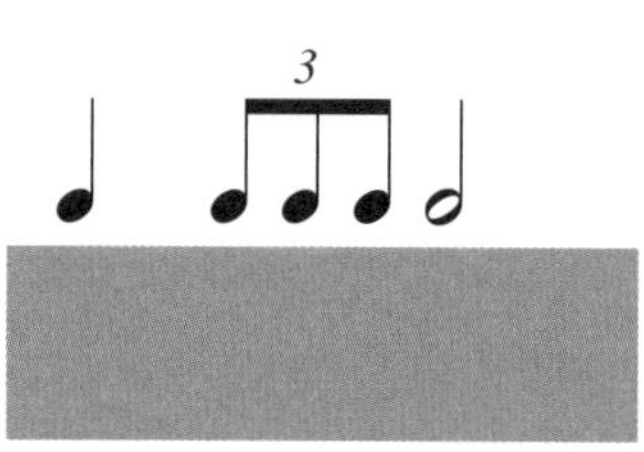

FLUTE PLAYER

ONE GALLOPING HORSE

DOWN BY THE STATION

EENCY WEENCY SPIDER

BABY BUGGY BABY BUGGY

CANDLE LIGHT CANDLE LIGHT

d.

e.

f.

Key of C Major

Strict march

1.

Key of A minor

Strict march

2.

Listening for 16th-note Rhythms

Your teacher will set a **steady beat** of **one full measure** and then tap either rhythm **a** or **b**. Circle **a** or **b** for the rhythm played.

1a. 

or

b. 

2a. 

or

b. 

3a. 

or

b. 

4a. 

or

b. 

Extra Credit: Tap an example for your teacher to identify, **a** or **b**.

Passacaglia (pronounced pah-suh-KAH-lyuh) is a famous piece by **George Frideric Handel**. Its musical form is marked by continuous **variations** with the character of a courtly dance.

Have fun and Take the Challenge!

New chord: B diminished

Play:

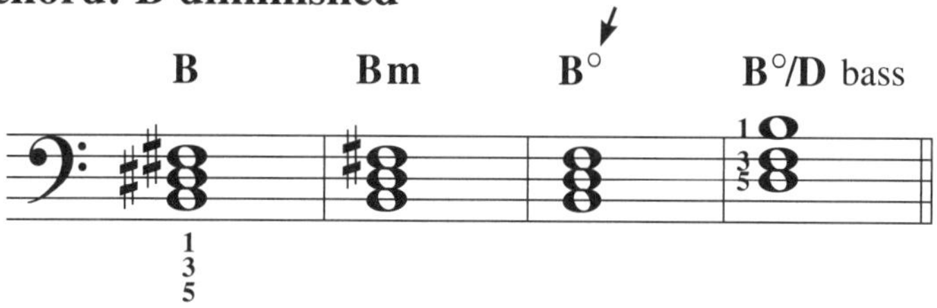

The small circle indicates **diminished**.
A diminished chord uses only **minor 3rds**.

Passacaglia*

Key of ___ Major/minor

THEME

George Frideric Handel
(1685-1759, Germany-England)
adapted

Dignified march tempo

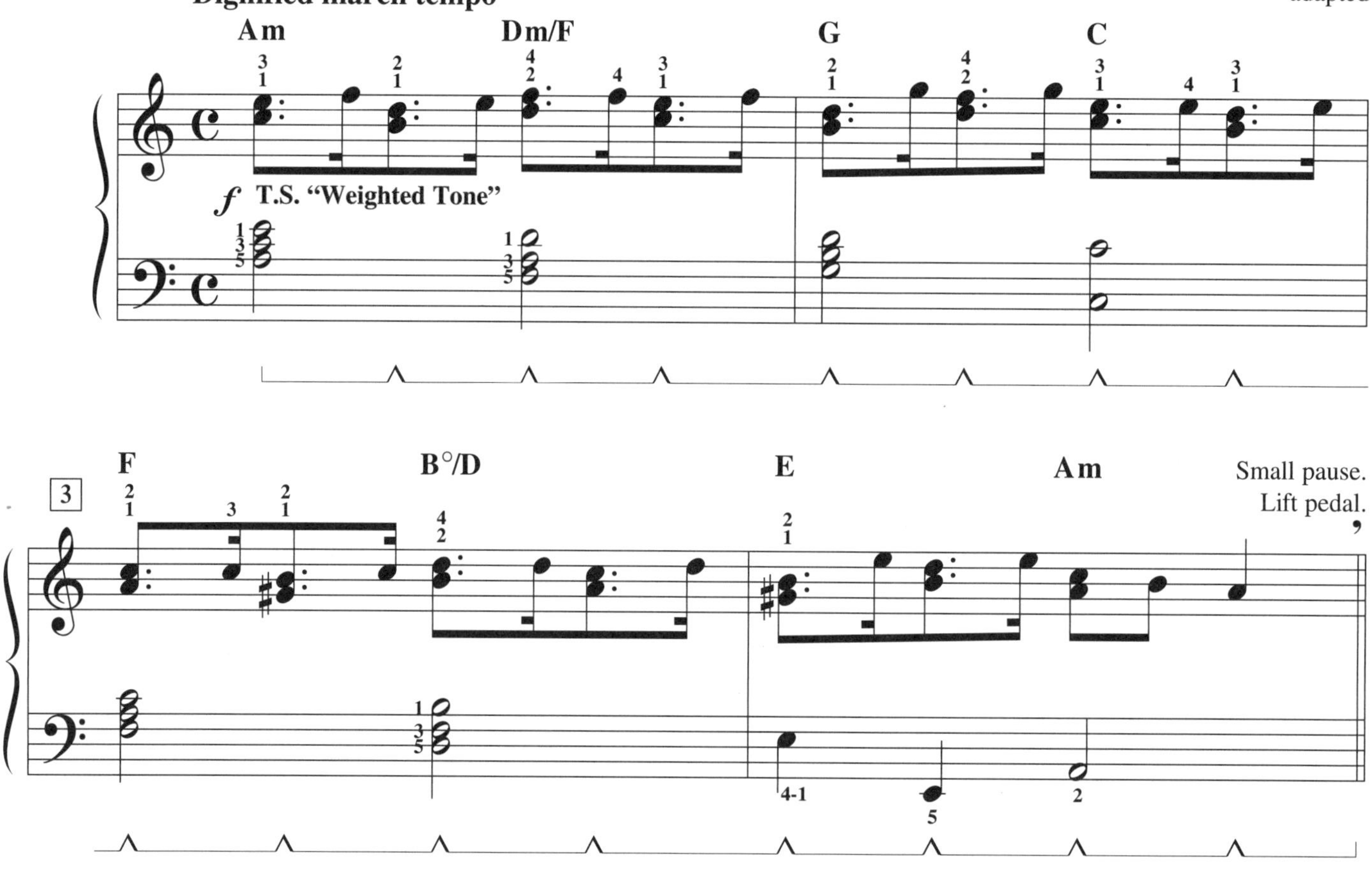

*from *Suite No. 7 in G minor.*

VARIATION 1

VARIATION 2

Rotation is a gentle side-to-side rocking motion of the hand—rather like turning a key in a lock. (Level 3A Technique Secret 3)

VARIATION 3

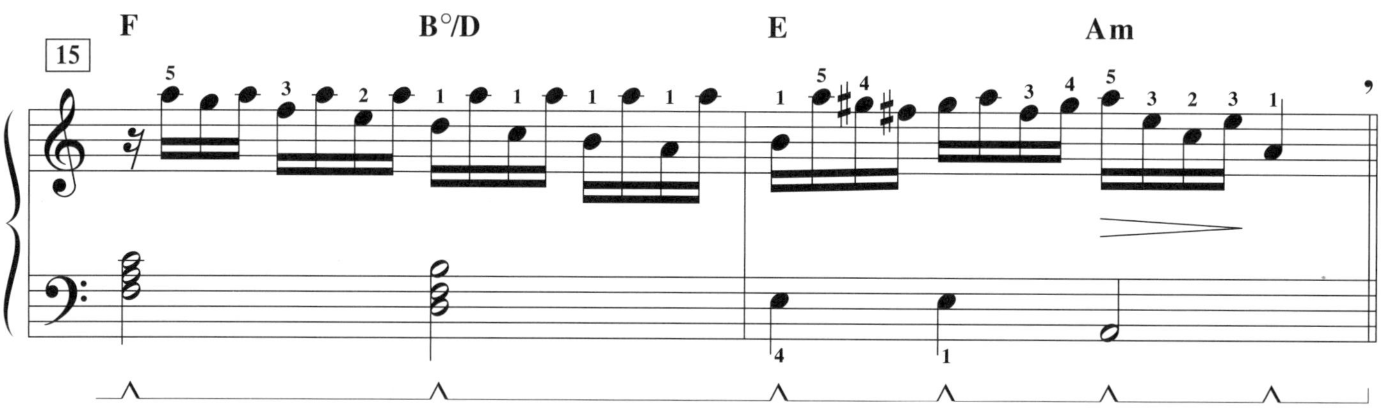

VARIATION 4

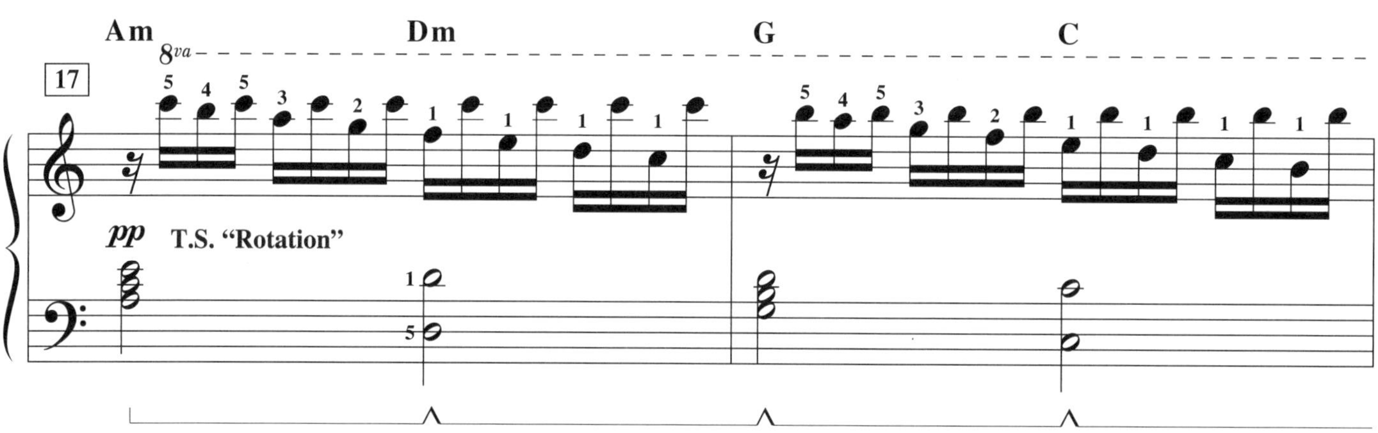

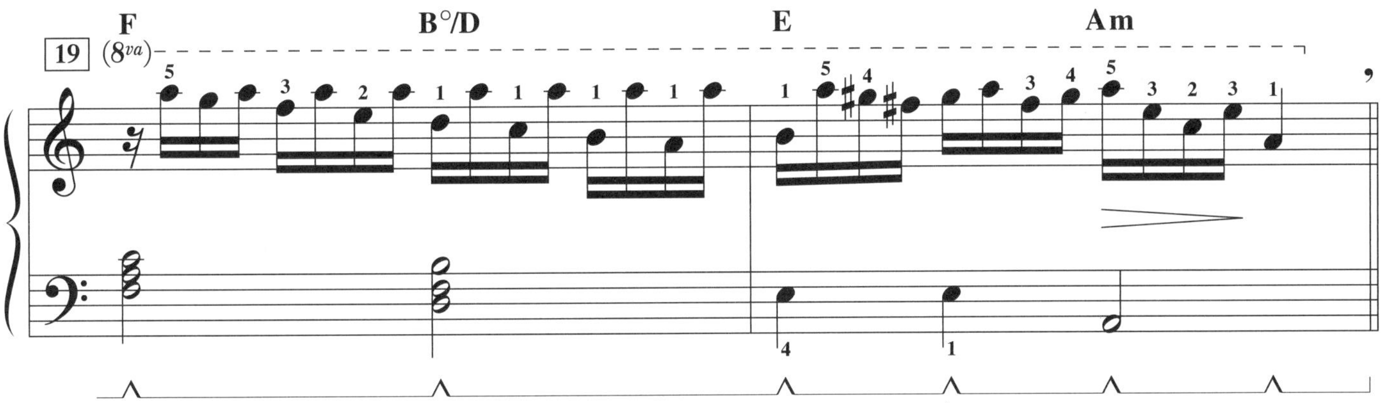

VARIATION 5

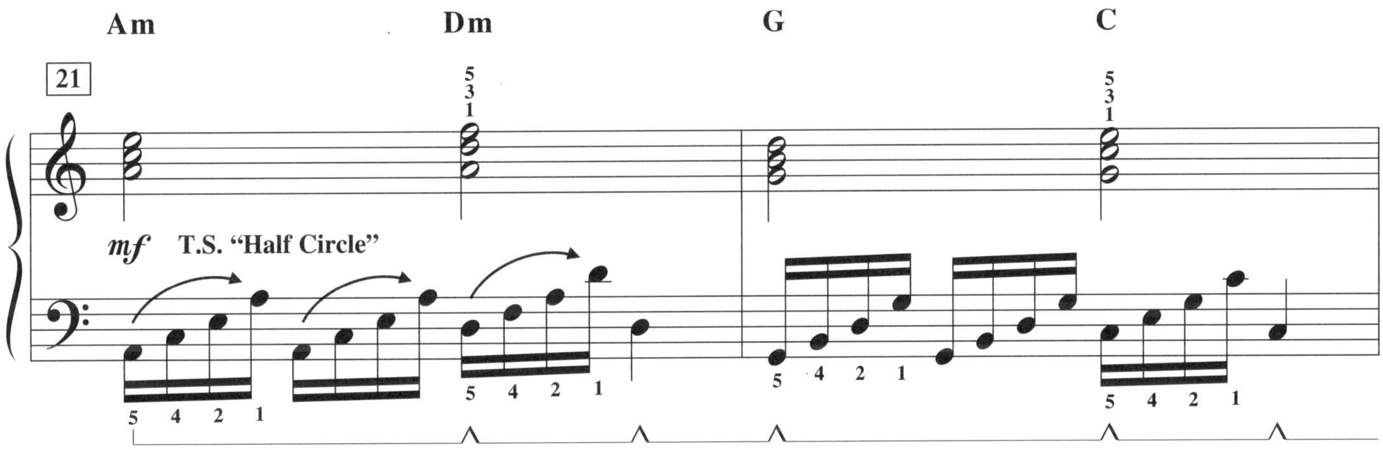

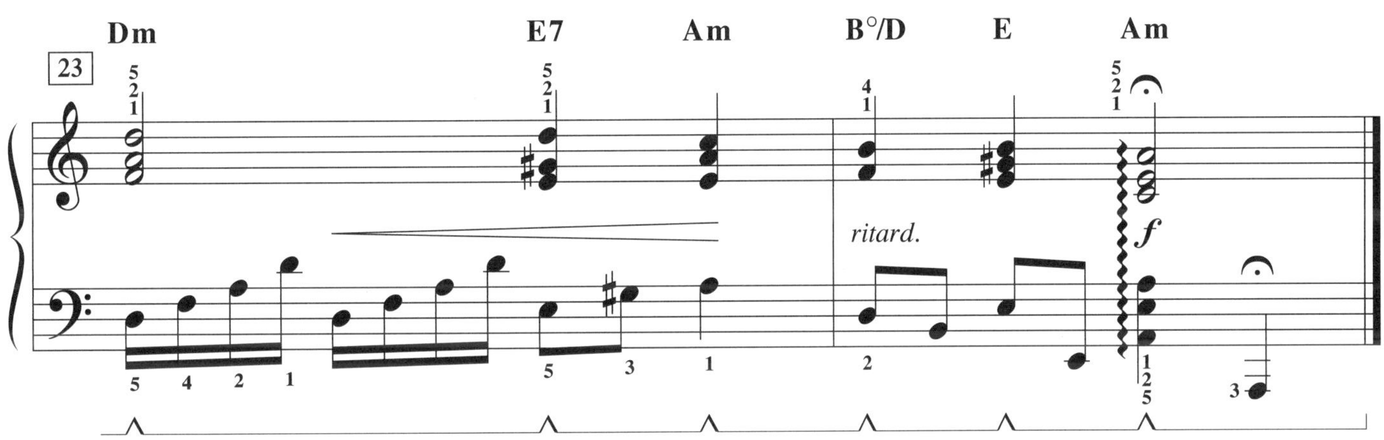

Balance on 3.
Keep wrist level.

2-Octave Scales: F Major and D Minor

Notice the "turn-around" that leads you to the **relative minor**.

LEARNING VIDEO

- Memorize each Scale Routine.

R.H. Scale Routine

F Major T.S. "Alignment"

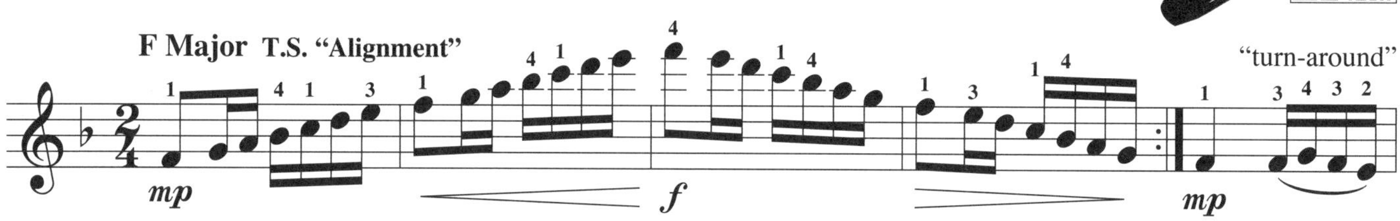

D Harmonic Minor

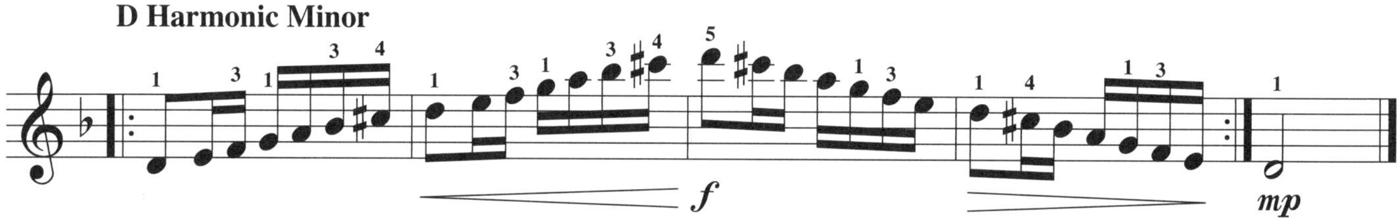

LEARNING VIDEO

L.H. Scale Routine

F Major T.S. "Alignment"

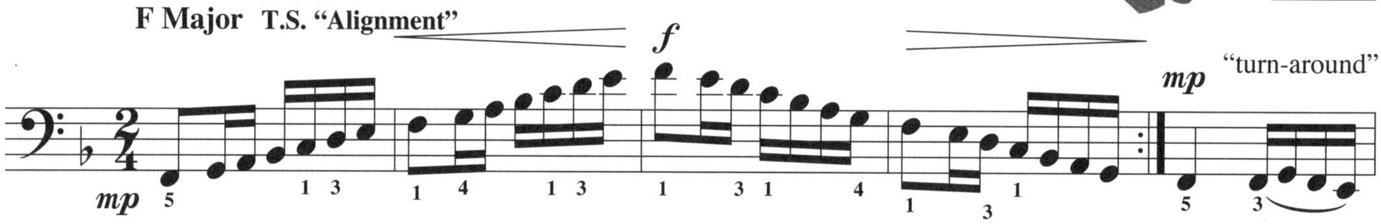

D Harmonic Minor

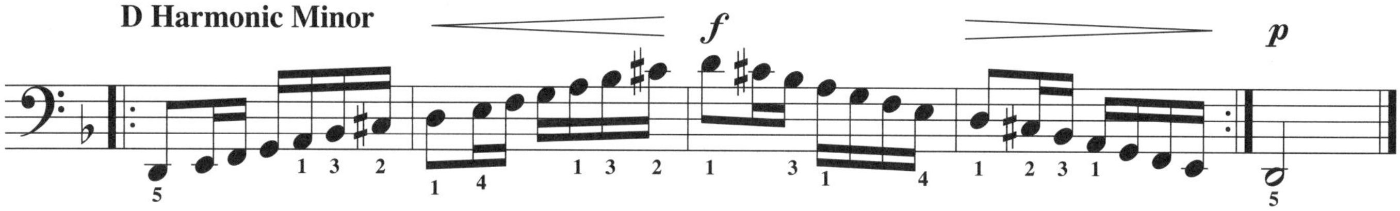

Optional: ____ ♩= 72 *Andante* ____ ♩= 100 *Moderato* ____ ♩= 112 *Allegro*

Find it Fast!

Remember, to quickly find the relative minor, count down **three half steps** from the *tonic* of the major key.

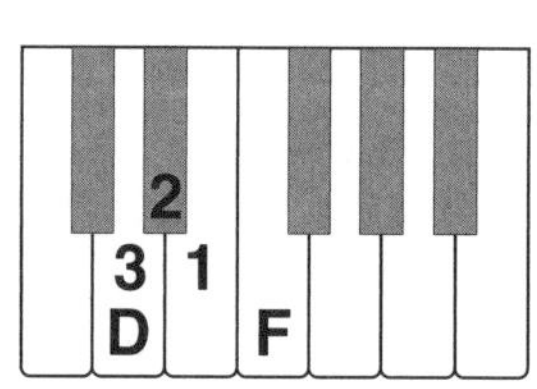

D minor is the relative minor of **F major**.

Review:
To find the **root** (chord name) of an inversion, locate the **interval of a 4th**.
The root will be the *upper note* of the **4th**.

You try!

The root is **F**.
F is the upper note of the **4th**.

The root is **D**.
D is the upper note of the **4th**.

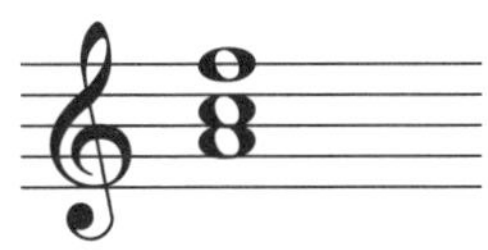

This root is ____.

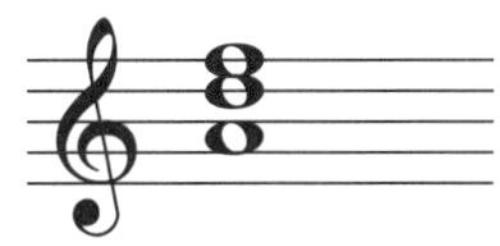

This root is ____.

LEARNING VIDEO

R.H. Chord Inversions

R.H. Broken Chords

F Major (F)

D Minor (Dm)

LEARNING VIDEO

L.H. Chord Inversions

L.H. Broken Chords

F Major (F)

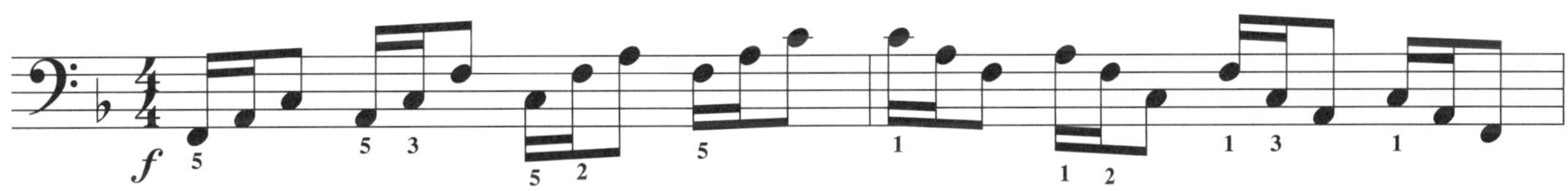

D Minor (Dm)

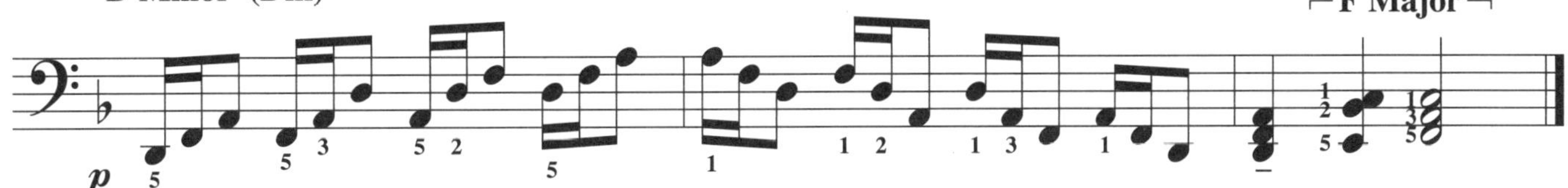

Key of F: Playing Root Position C7 Chords

LEARNING VIDEO

• Learn this L.H. Etude. Sing or say the words.

L.H. Harmony Etude: F-C7 Chords

LEARNING VIDEO

• The **letter names** and **Roman numerals** are written for measures 4-5. Write the harmony in for the rest of the **blue boxes**.

Mazurka in F Major*

Allegretto

N. Faber

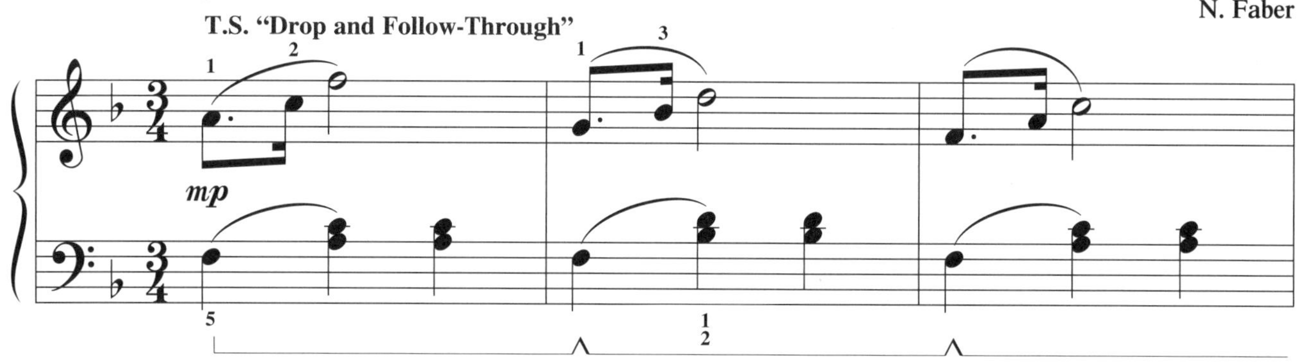

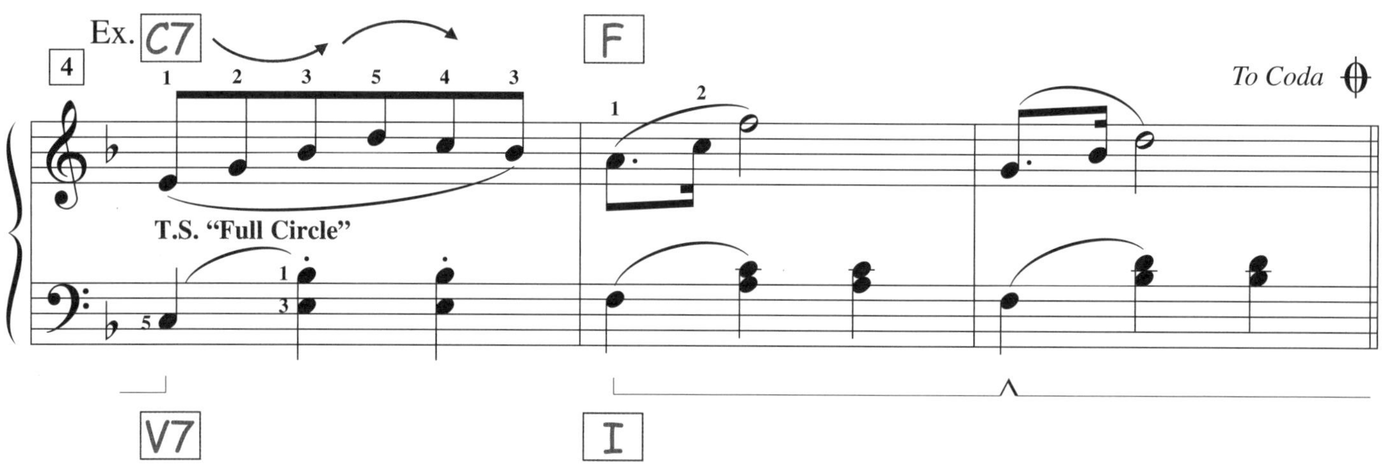

* A lively Polish dance in 3/4 time.

*tempestuous, stormy

Writing F Major and D Minor Scales

THEORY

Thinking in F Major and D Minor

1. Remember, to find the relative minor key, count down **three half steps** from the *tonic* of the major key.

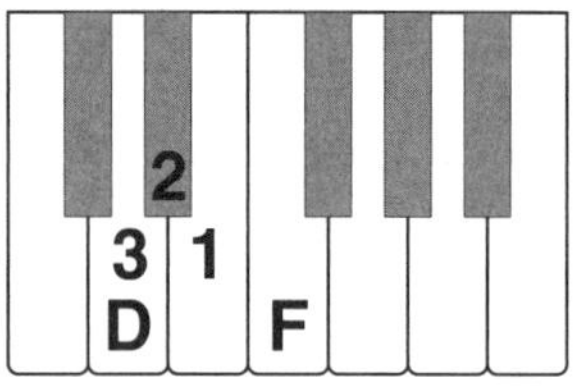

D minor is the relative minor of **F major**.

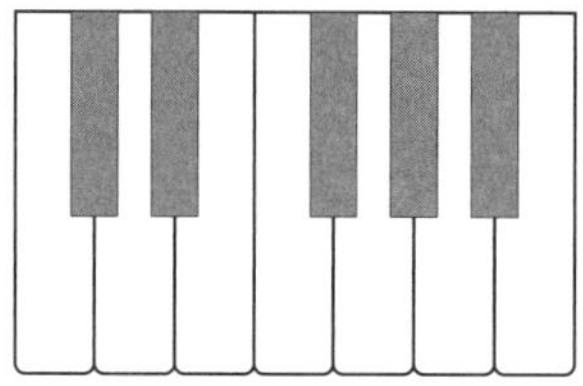

- Copy the example to the left.

2.
- Draw the key signature for **F major**. (See p. 58, if needed.)
- Write a **one-octave F major scale** ascending and descending. Use whole notes.
- Shade and label the *tonic* (**T**), *dominant* (**D**), and *leading tone* (**LT**).

key signature

R.H.

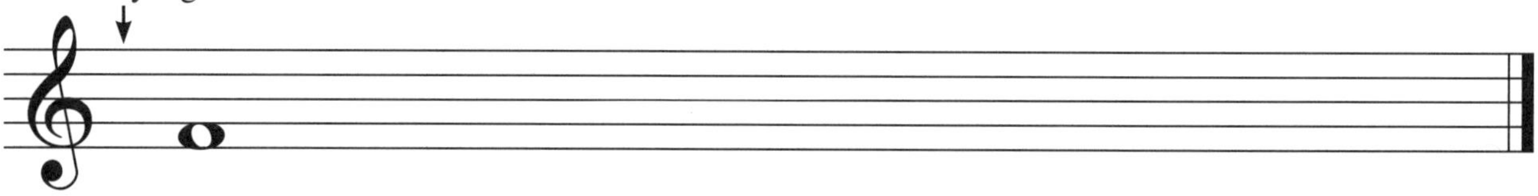

key signature

L.H.

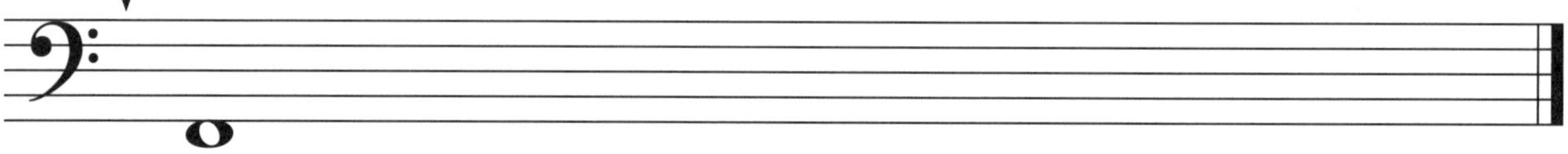

3.
- Draw the key signature for **D minor**. (See p. 58, if needed.)
- Write a **one-octave D harmonic minor scale** ascending and descending. Remember the C♯!
- Shade and label the *tonic* (**T**), *dominant* (**D**), and *leading tone* (**LT**).

key signature

R.H.

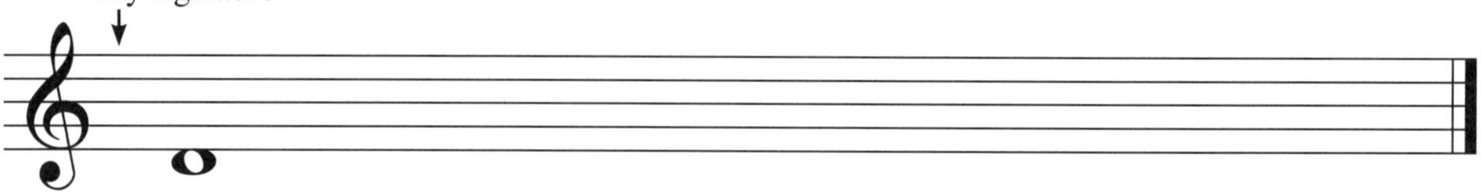

key signature

L.H.

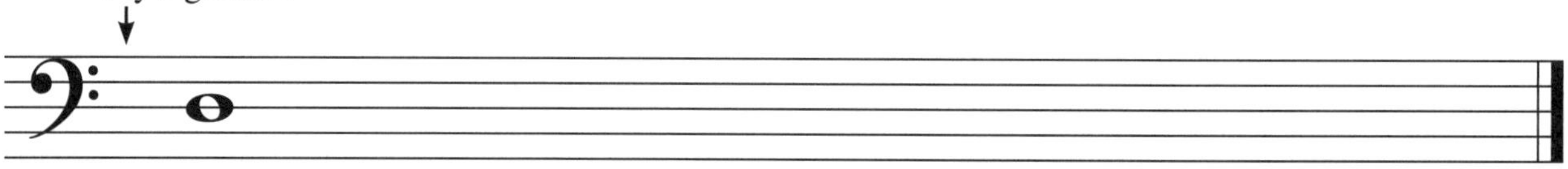

Review: **Tonic** refers to **step 1** of the scale. **Dominant** refers to **step 5** of the scale.

Key of F major:

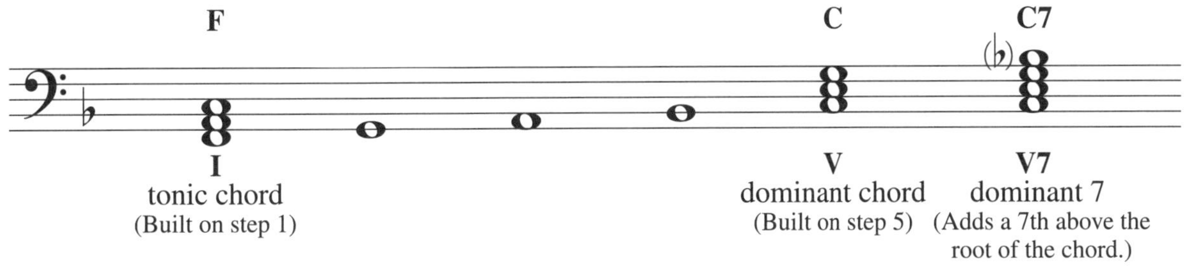

- Write **F** or **C7** in the boxes above the staff. Write **I** or **V7** in the boxes below the staff.
- Circle **no 3rd/5th** where indicated.
- Now play the melody and chords hands together.

The Trout

Franz Schubert
(1797-1828)
arranged

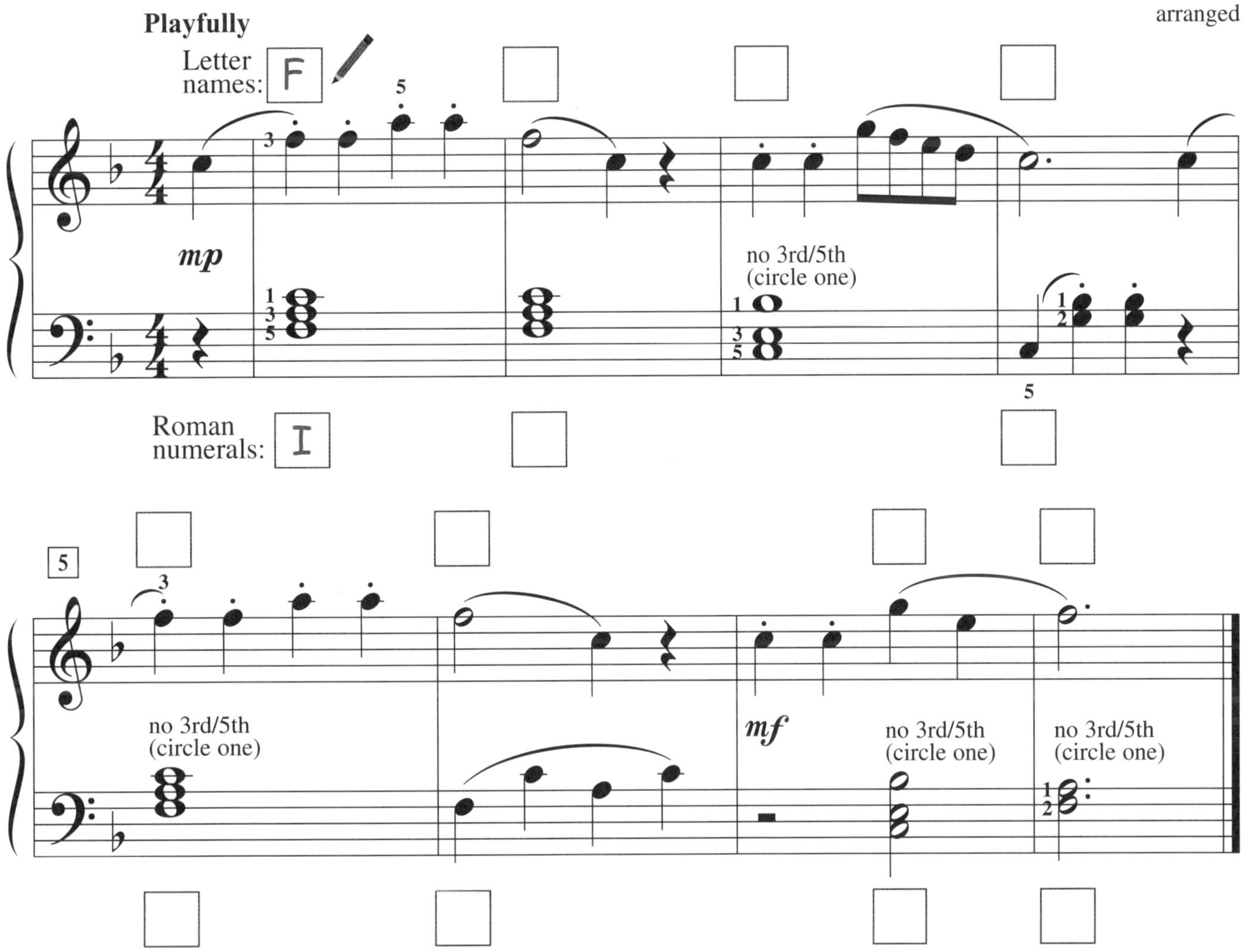

LEARNING VIDEO

- Learn this L.H. Etude. Sing or say the words. Notice that the **V** and **V7** chords are **major**, even in a **minor key**.

L.H. Harmony Etude: Dm-A7 Chords

LEARNING VIDEO

Review: Ostinato
This Italian word literally means "stubborn."

Ostinato is a persistently **repeating phrase**.
Imagine the spy determined to solve the case!

The Spy

N. Faber

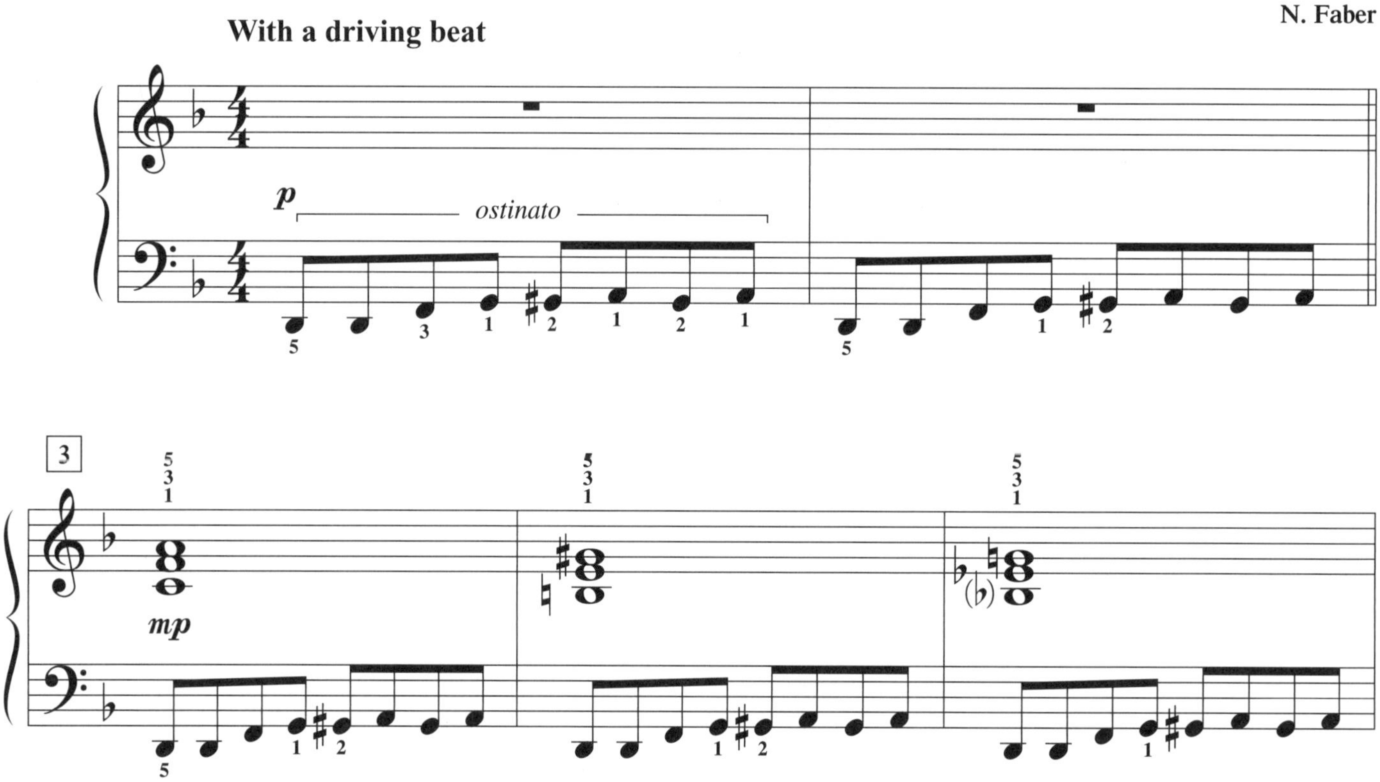

6
9
A7 Dm
mf
V7 i
12
14
p
17
1.
A7
2.
V7

20
f
dim. poco a poco
23
26
p
mp
29
sfz
(top note optional)
f
33
ff
(prepare L.H.)
sfz
8va

Remember, to **improvise**, we often create sounds using a **specific scale**.

1. • First, learn this **F major accompaniment**.
Play while your teacher *improvises* a melody higher using notes from the **F major scale**.

• Now you **improvise**! (Teacher plays duet.)

F improv
Walk at Dawn

LEARNING VIDEO

Adventure Quote | *"Logic will get you from A to Z. Imagination will get you anywhere." –Albert Einstein*

2. • Next, learn this **D minor accompaniment**.
Play while your teacher *improvises* a melody higher using notes from the **D harmonic minor scale**.

• Now you **improvise**! (Teacher plays duet.)

Dm IMPROV
Firelight Dance

LEARNING VIDEO

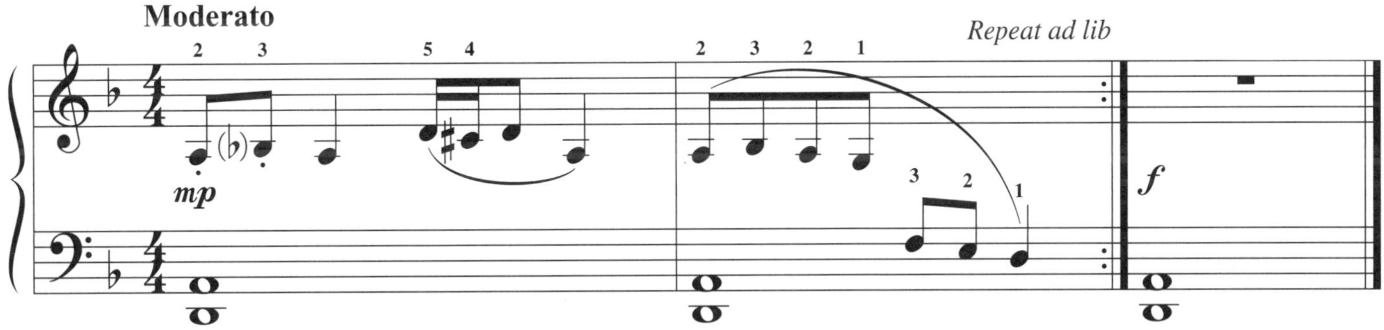

Andantino
A little faster than *andante* (walking speed)

Lully composed for King Louis XIV. The King would often dance to Lully's music. This piece is from the **Baroque Period** (1600-1750), a time of glittering courts, wigs on men, and a decorative style of art and architecture.

BAROQUE BAROQUE LEARNING VIDEO

French Minuet

Key of ___ Major/minor

Jean-Baptiste Lully
(1632-1687, France)
original form

Andantino T.S. "Alignment"

DISCOVERY Where does Lully's minuet go to the **relative major**? *measure* ____
The form of this piece is binary. Label the parts in your music.

- Play the L.H. broken chords saying I, **IV**, or **V7**. Mozart was one of the major composers from the **Classical Period** (1750-1830); a time of elegance, simplicity and less grandeur than the Baroque.

Dance in F Major

LEARNING VIDEO

Wolfgang Amadeus Mozart
(1756-1791, Germany)
original form

Irving Berlin's music has come to occupy a major portion of **The Great American Songbook**—those jazz and popular songs that contributed significantly to the culture. You may recognize these other Berlin titles as well: "White Christmas," "There's No Business Like Show Business," and "Alexander's Ragtime Band," to name a few.

Puttin' on the Ritz

Key of ___ Major/minor

Irving Berlin
(1888-1989, USA)
arranged

Adventure Quote | *"Attitudes are a secret power working twenty-four hours a day. It is of paramount importance that we know how to harness and control this great force." -Irving Berlin*

Analyze the Chords: Dm, A, and A7

THEORY

Review: **Tonic** refers to **step 1** of the scale. **Dominant** refers to **step 5** of the scale.

Key of D minor:

Dm — **A** — **A7**

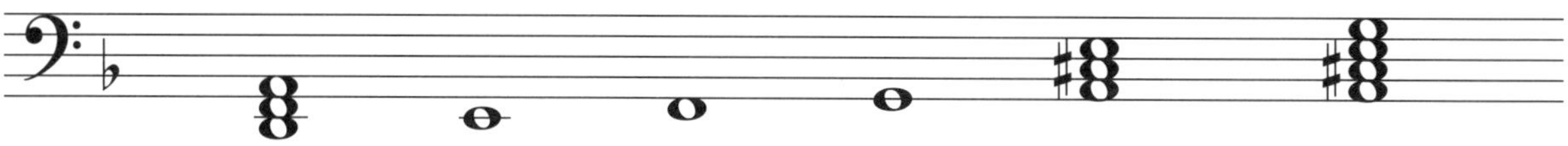

i tonic chord (Built on step 1)

V dominant chord (Built on step 5)

V7 dominant 7 (Adds a 7th above the root of the chord.)

Analyze each chord in **D minor**.

- Write letter names **Dm**, **A**, or **A7** *above* the staff.
- Write Roman numerals **i**, **V**, or **V7** *below* the staff.

Chord Sleuth

Ex.

letter names: Dm

1. 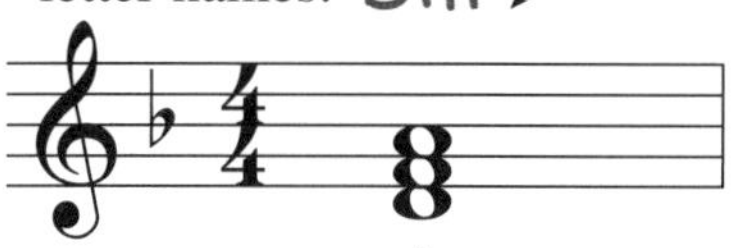

Roman numerals: i

Ex.

A

2. 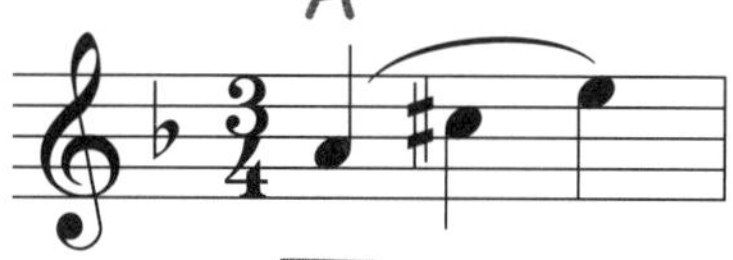

V

3. 

4. 

5. 

6. 

7. 

8. 

9. 

10. 

11. 

12. 

THEORY

- Write the following chords in **root position**, **1st inversion**, and **2nd inversion**.
- Can you play these chords and inversions on the keyboard?

Notice the ledger lines.

C major

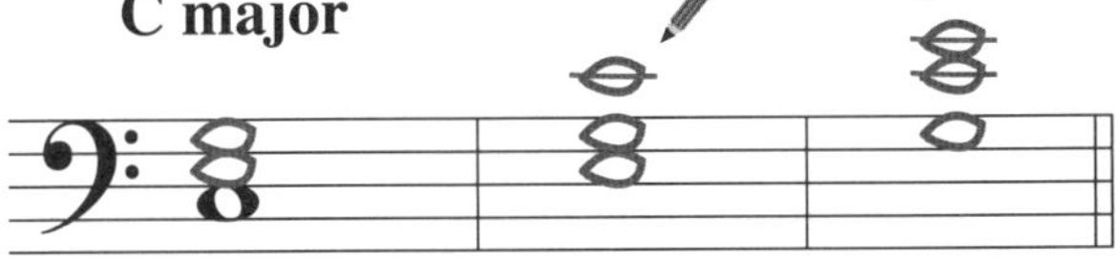

Ex. root position | 1st inversion | 2nd inversion

C major

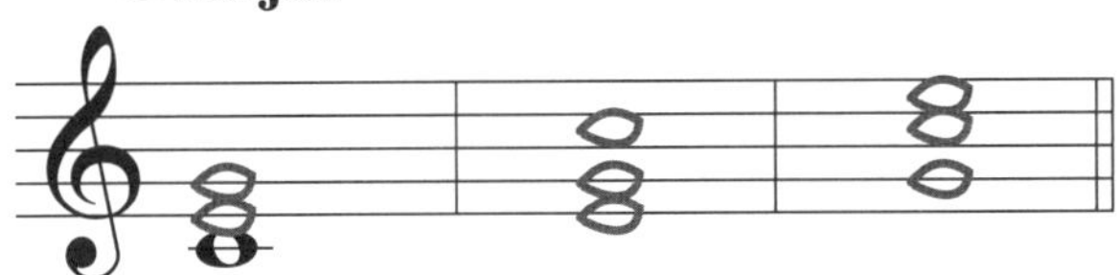

Ex. root position | 1st inversion | 2nd inversion

F major

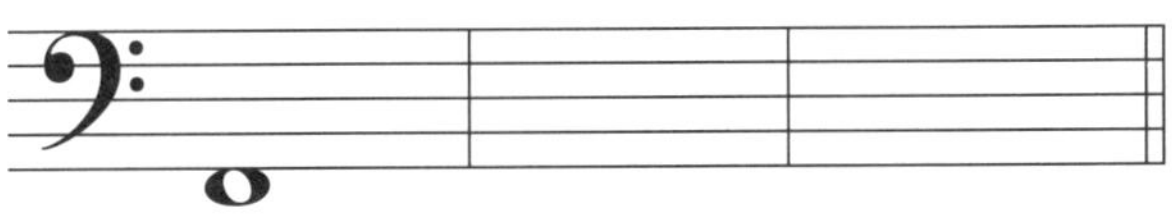

root position | 1st inversion | 2nd inversion

F major (Use ledger lines.)

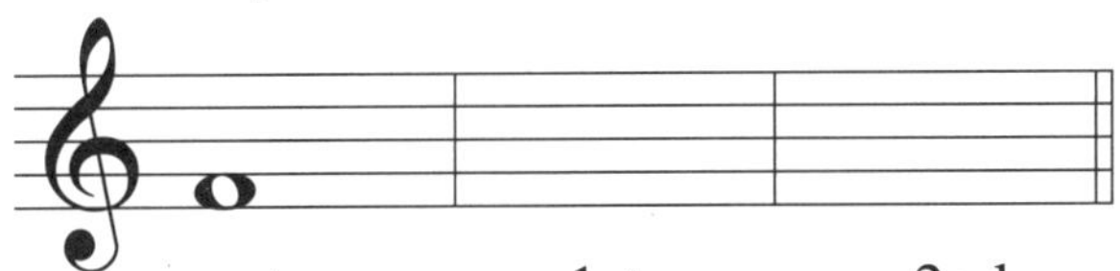

root position | 1st inversion | 2nd inversion

D minor

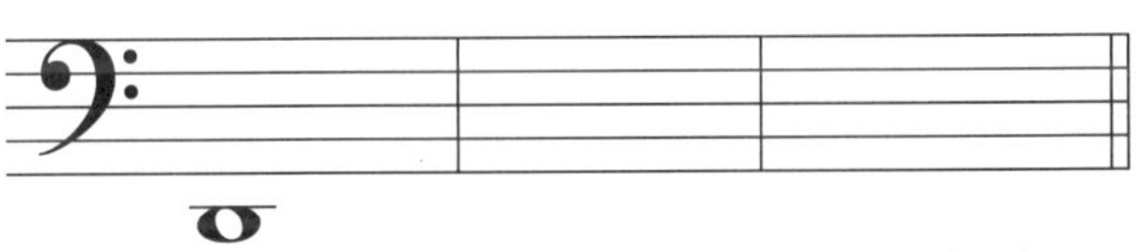

root position | 1st inversion | 2nd inversion

D minor

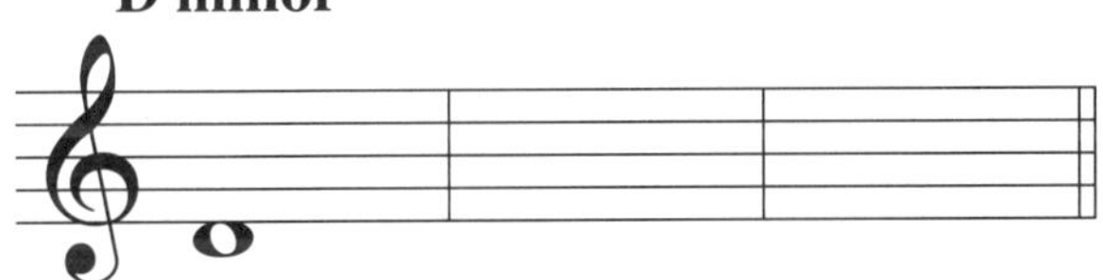

root position | 1st inversion | 2nd inversion

C major (Use ledger lines.)

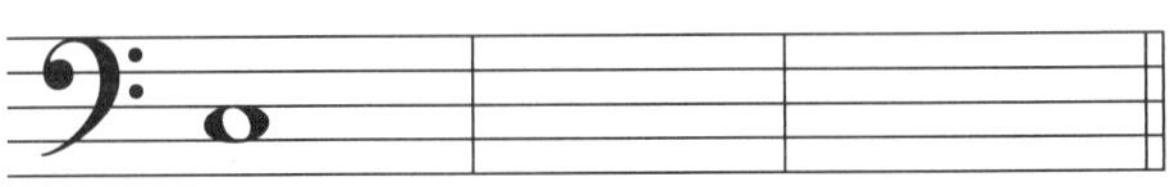

root position | 1st inversion | 2nd inversion

C major

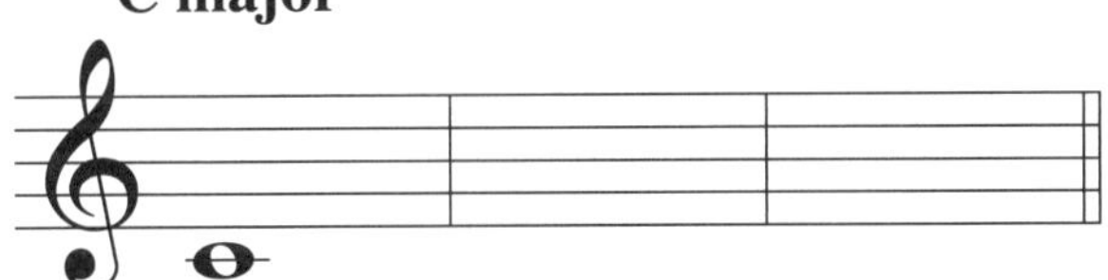

root position | 1st inversion | 2nd inversion

A minor

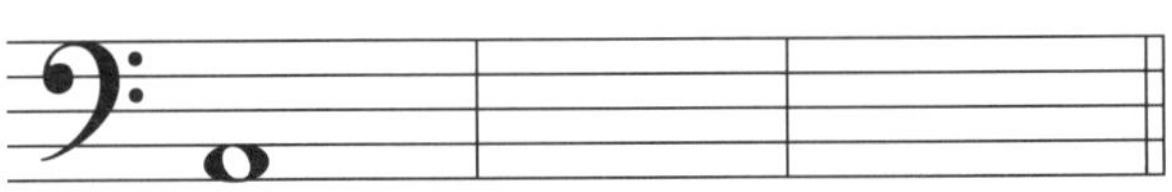

root position | 1st inversion | 2nd inversion

A minor (Use ledger lines.)

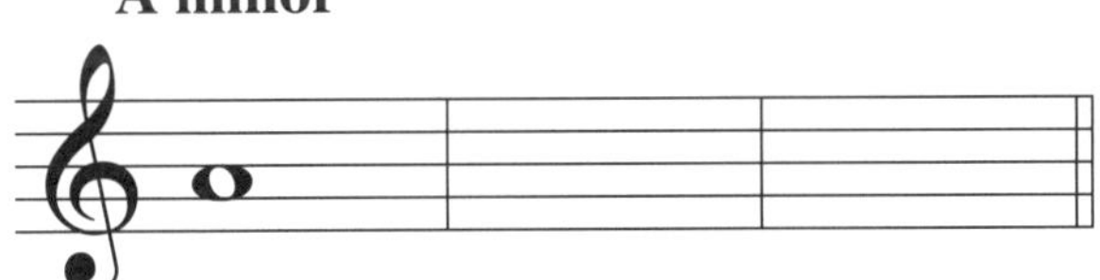

root position | 1st inversion | 2nd inversion

Key of Dm: Creating Tonal Colors

Silver Rain Etude has many TONAL COLORS, from the opening ***piano*** to the final ***forte***.

- First learn the notes and fingering. Finding **patterns** will help you. Can you find a broken chord pattern for the **A7** chord?
- Vary your weighted touch to match the **dynamics**.
- Review: For *measures 8-9*, use **rotation**, a back and forth rocking motion of the hand. (Rotation is a Technique Secret taught in Level 3A.)

LEARNING VIDEO

Silver Rain Etude

Key of ____ Major/minor

Allegro (♩ = 88-100)

N. Faber

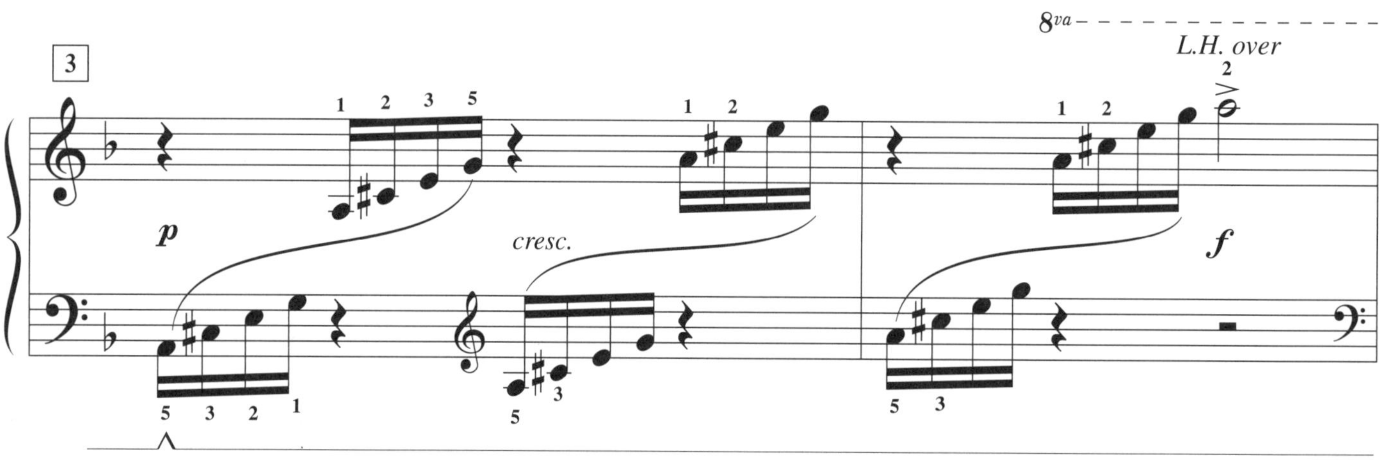

(8va)
5
(f)
mf
7
mp
poco rit.
a tempo
mf
9
mp
p
freely
11
8va
rit.
pp
Slowly
f

LEARNING VIDEO

Gustav Holst's most famous work is his orchestral suite called **"The Planets."** This arrangement of the movement **"Jupiter"** has a majestic melody with dignified L.H. octaves.

Have fun and Take the Challenge!

Jupiter

Key of ____ Major/minor

Gustav Holst
(1874-1934, England)
arranged

Slowly, dignified

Adventure Quote | "The music of 'The Planets' enables the mind to acquire some comprehension of the vastness of space where rational understanding fails." –Gustav Holst

2-Octave Scales: G Major and E minor

Notice the "turn-around" that leads you to the **relative minor**.

- Memorize each Scale Routine.

R.H. Scale Routine

LEARNING VIDEO

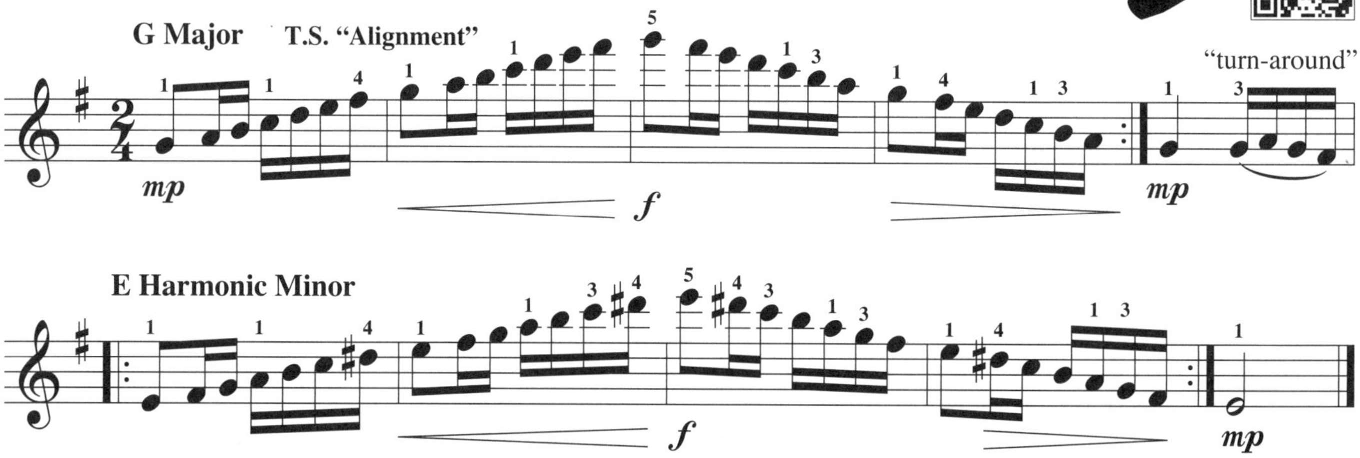

L.H. Scale Routine

LEARNING VIDEO

____ ♩ = 72 *Andante* ____ ♩ = 100 *Moderato* ____ ♩ = 112 *Allegro*

Find it Fast!

Remember, to quickly find the relative minor, count down **three half steps** from the *tonic* of the major key.

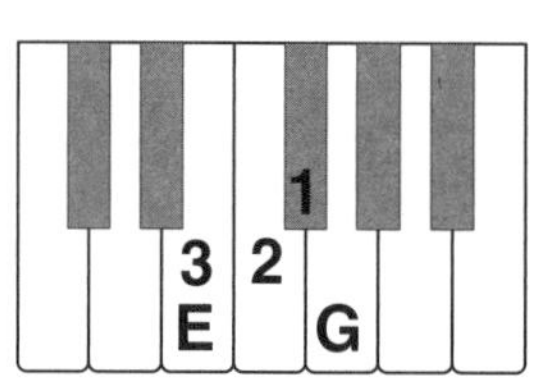

E minor is the relative minor of **G major**.

- Play at a **quick tempo**.

Rhythm Hint: You do not need to count "**1 e and a**." Simply play the **16th note** very quickly into the **quarter note** that follows.

LEARNING VIDEO

R.H. Chord Inversions

R.H. Broken and Blocked Chords

LEARNING VIDEO

L.H. Chord Inversions

L.H. Broken and Blocked Chords

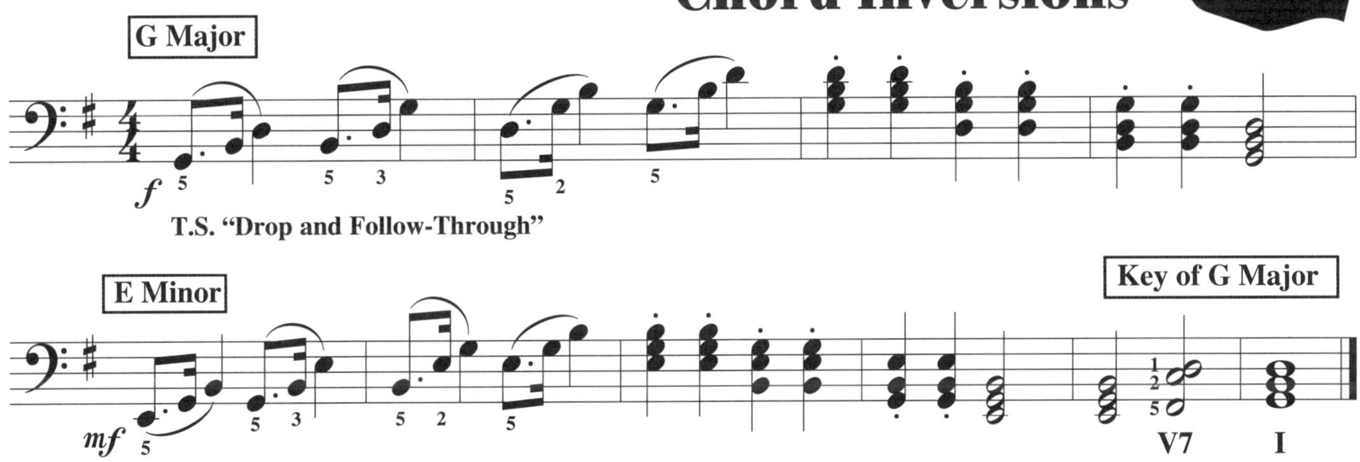

DISCOVERY

Can you play each **chord inversion exercise** from memory?

TECHNIQUE

TECHNIQUE SECRET 4
Half Circle/Full Circle, p.15

LEARNING VIDEO

Brushstrokes
(L.H. alone)

- Pivot on **finger 2** for a smooth, relaxed gesture.
- Play the **thumb** *lightly* with a rising wrist.

LEARNING VIDEO

TECHNIQUE SECRET 4
Half Circle/Full Circle, p.15

Often a composer uses the **major key** and its **relative minor key** in the same piece.

- The form of this piece is **ABA.**
  Name the key used in each section: ____ ____ ____
  A **B** **A**

Chanson*

Flowing, expressively

N. Faber

Chanson is the French word for "song."

17
mp
21
mf
25
29
f
mf
mp poco rit.
p
a tempo
33
mp

Adventure Quote | *"A piano is a canvas, and the pianist is the artist painting emotions with every stroke of the keys." -Anonymous*

CREATIVE Compose a 4-measure melody in G major.
Can you play your melody in the relative minor (E minor)?

Key of G: Root Position D7 Chord

• Learn this L.H. Etude. Sing or say the words.

LEARNING VIDEO

L.H. Harmony Etude: G-D7 Chords

LEARNING VIDEO

Review: Grace note
An ornamental note played quickly into the note that follows. See *measure 4.*

Grand Central Station

N. Faber

Adventure Quote | *"Rhythm takes us on a grand tour of melody and harmony through its magnificent motion." -Anonymous*

Writing G Major and E Minor Scales

THEORY

Thinking in G Major and E Minor

1. Complete the rule: To find the relative minor key, count down _____ **half steps** from the __________ of the major key.

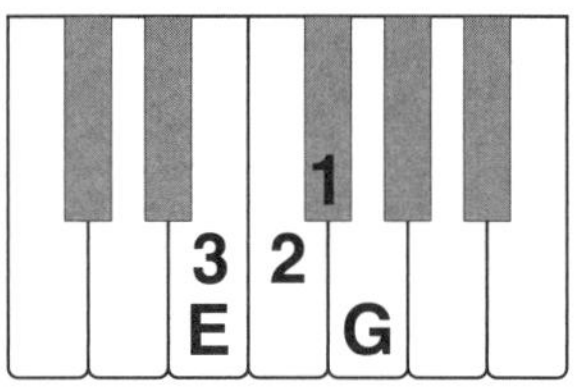

E minor is the relative minor of **G major**.

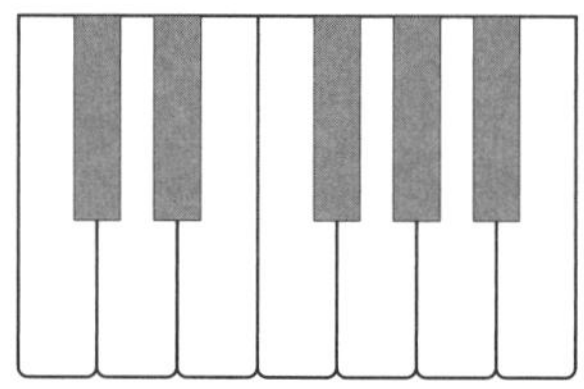

- **Copy** the example to the left.

2.
- Draw the key signature for **G major**. (See p. 78, if needed.)
- Write a **one-octave G major scale** ascending and descending. Use whole notes.
- Shade and label the *tonic* (**T**), *dominant* (**D**), and *leading tone* (**LT**).

3.
- Draw the key signature for **E minor**. (See p. 78, if needed.)
- Write a **one-octave E harmonic minor scale** ascending and descending. Remember the D♯!
- Shade and label the *tonic* (**T**), *dominant* (**D**), and *leading tone* (**LT**).

Review: **Tonic** refers to **step 1** of the scale. **Dominant** refers to **step 5** of the scale.

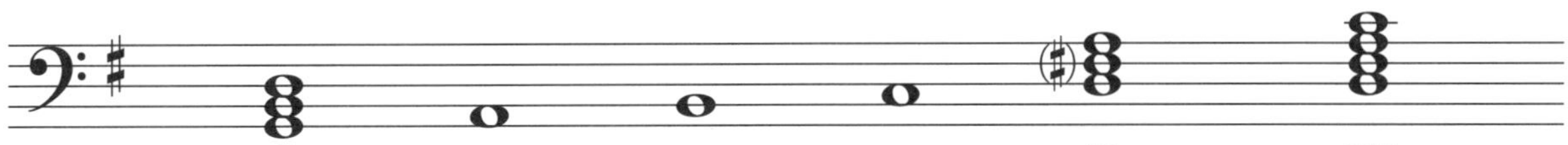

LEARNING VIDEO

- Write **G** or **D7** in the boxes *above* the staff.
  Write **I** or **V7** in the boxes *below* the staff.
- Circle **no 3rd/5th** where indicated.
- Now play the melody and chords hands together.

Allegro Melody

Mauro Giuliani
(1781-1829, Italy)
arranged

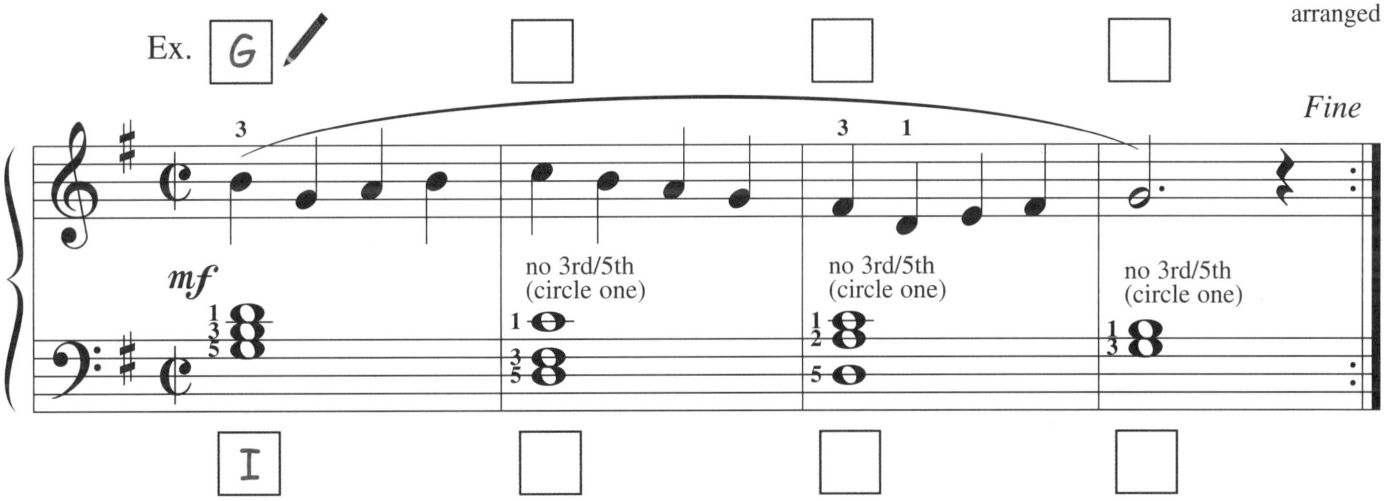

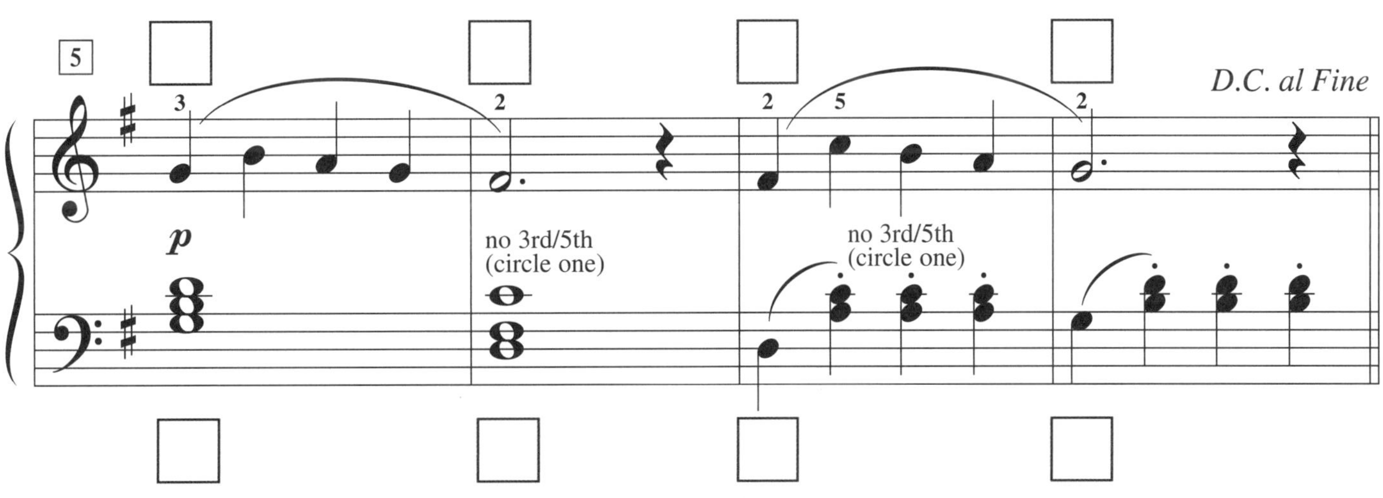

- Learn this L.H. Etude. Sing or say the words.

LEARNING VIDEO

L.H. Harmony Etude: Em-B7 Chords

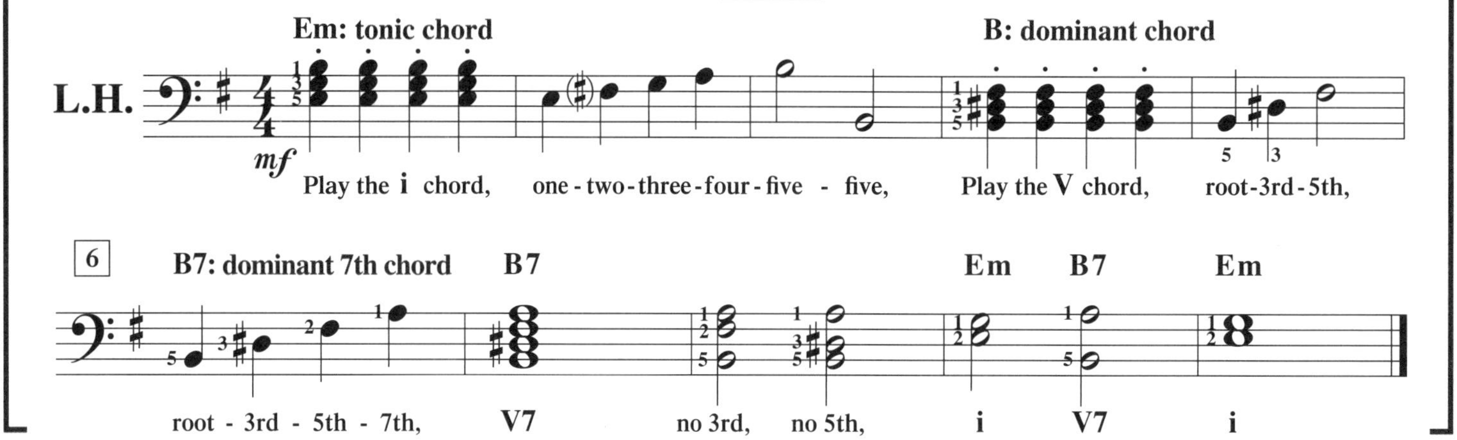

LEARNING VIDEO

Volga Boatmen

Traditional

trill (*tr*) – a rapid alternation between two neighboring notes. (Teacher demonstrates.)

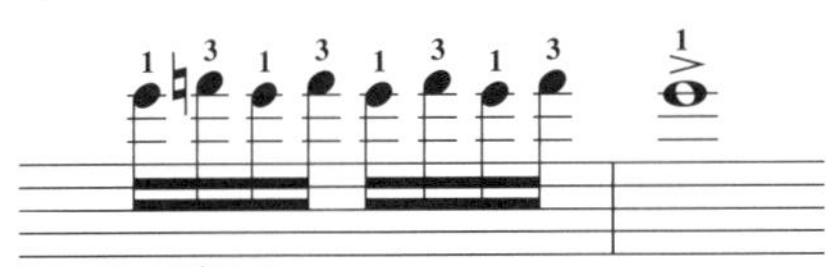

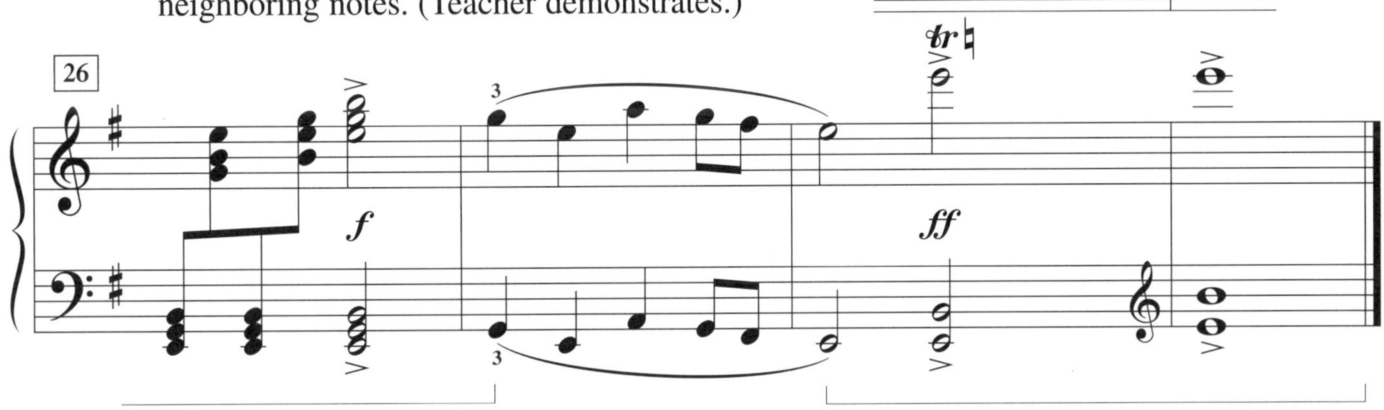

Composing a Waltz in E Minor

THEORY

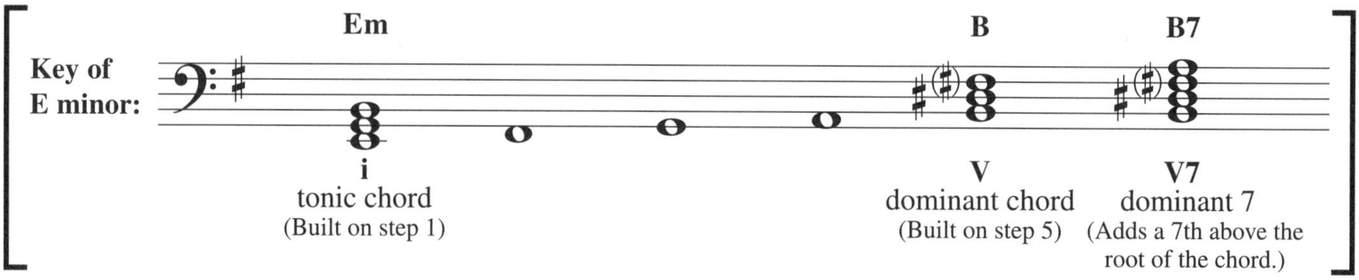

This piece is in **A B A form**. It begins in the key of **E minor** and moves to the *relative major* (**G major**) for the B section.

- First play the L.H. "waltz" chords, writing **i**, **I**, or **V7** in the boxes.
- Then **compose a R.H. melody**. Use the sample rhythm given or create your own. Hint: Use mainly chord tones and let your ear guide you.
- Play your composition! Can you transpose to **D minor** (and **F major**)?

LEARNING VIDEO

Minor-Major Waltz

Allegretto

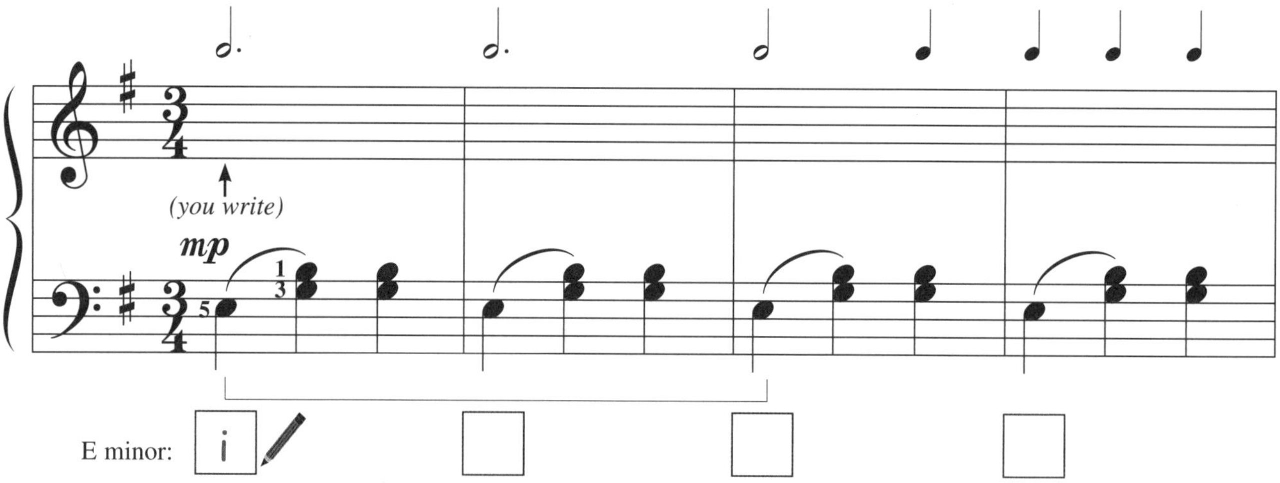

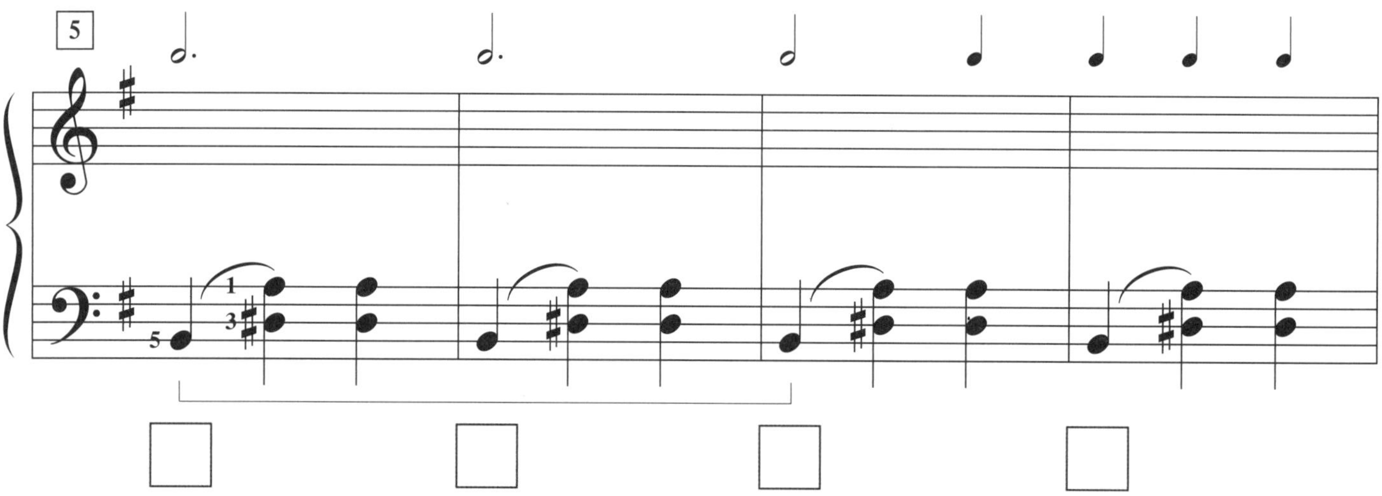

9
13
Fine
17
B section
mf
New key:
____ major
(fill in)
I
22
1.
2.
D.C. al Fine
rit.
p

LEARNING VIDEO

Seaside Suite

1. Sailboats in the Wind

Key of ___ Major/minor

Moving quickly (♩ = 116-132)

N. Faber

13
mf
16
a tempo
f
poco rit.
p
cross
over
19
22
poco rit.
a tempo
mp
lift
25
8va
rit.
pp

Review:
trill (*tr*) - a rapid alternation between two neighboring notes.

- Can you find the **trill** in this piece?

LEARNING VIDEO

2. Mysterious Cove

Key of ___ Major/minor

Slow and mysterious (♩. = 60-69)

13
mf
cross 2 over
16
19
f
mp
8va
22
p
25
pp
tr
8va

LEARNING VIDEO

This last movement uses R.H. **2nd inversion chords**.

- Keep your hand in a relaxed, but molded position to play the consecutive **2nd inversion chords**.

3. Surfboards

Key of ___ Major/minor

*Students with larger hands may enjoy playing an octave here.

DISCOVERY Name the **root** of the first four R.H. chords. (Hint: Remember to look for the upper note of each 4th.) Is each chord *major* or *minor?*

- Notice the **R.H.** has "**two voices**" at *measures 7, 10, 11, 15.* Your teacher will demonstrate.
- Hint: First practice hands separately.

Bourrée

Key of ___ minor

Christoph Graupner
(1683-1760, Germany)
original form

Moderato

Is the form Binary ‖: A :‖: B :‖ or Rounded Binary ‖: A :‖: B A :‖ ?

Adventure Quote | *"I live my daydreams in music." -Albert Einstein*

1. • First, write the **chord letter name** (G or Em) in each box.

• Learn this **G major accompaniment**. Play while your teacher *improvises* a **melody** higher using notes from the **G major scale**.

• Now you **improvise**! (Teacher plays duet.)

LEARNING VIDEO

G IMPROV
Rhythm Bop!

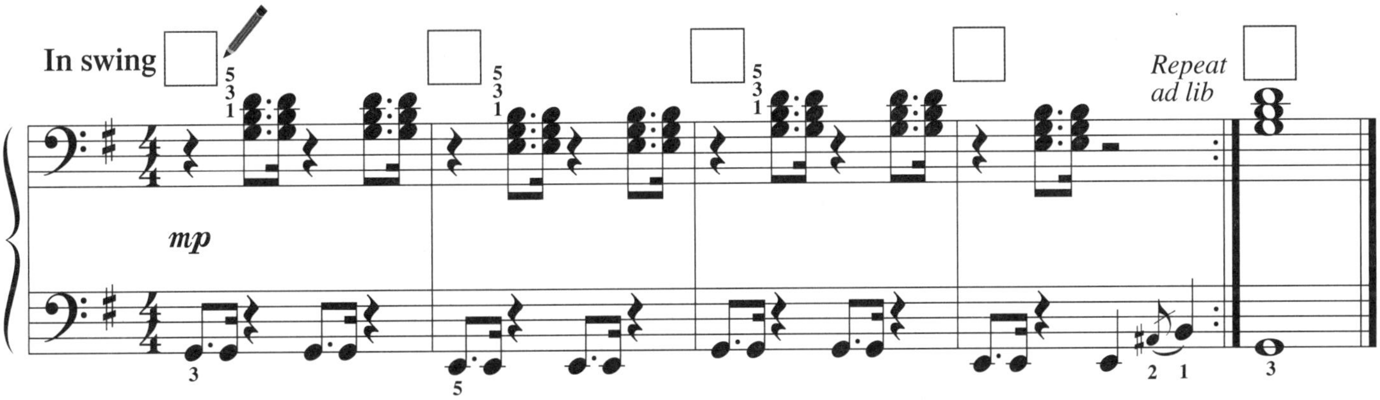

2. • Next, learn this **E minor accompaniment**. Play while your teacher *improvises* a melody higher using notes from the **E harmonic minor scale**.

• Now you **improvise**! (Teacher plays duet.)

LEARNING VIDEO

Em IMPROV
misty lagoon

3. Write the **chord letter name**; then circle root position, 1st inversion, or 2nd inversion.

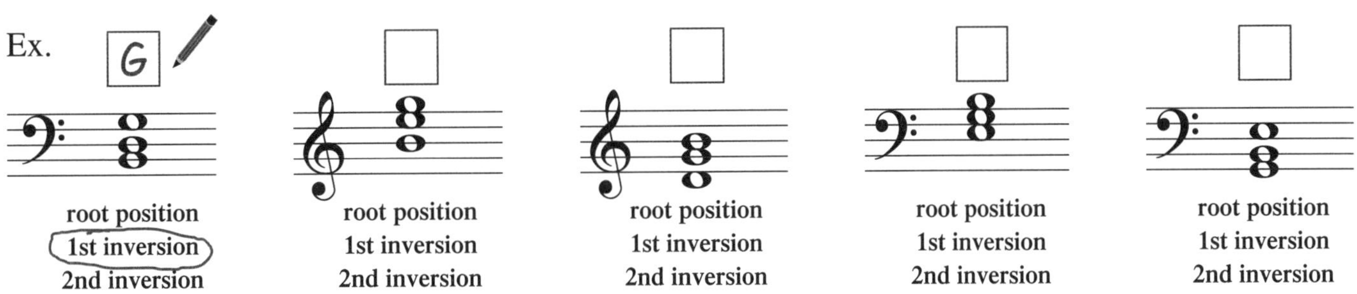

The **bolero** is a Spanish dance. **Maurice Ravel's** famous "Bolero" features a lovely, enchanting melody with a **L.H. accompaniment** that **repeats** over and over. The piece leads to a dramatic and rhythmically exciting conclusion.

Have fun and Take the Challenge!

Bolero

Key of ____Major/minor

Maurice Ravel
(1875-1937, France)
arranged

13
15
To Coda
18
21
f

24
lift
mp
26
TRI - PO - LET 2 + a 3 + a
28
30
1 + 2 + TRI - PO - LET
32

34
36
D.S. 𝄋 al Coda
(R.H. moves 8va)
Coda
loco
T.S. "Drop and Follow-Through"
41
43
broaden
shift

Sharp Key Signatures

To name a key signature with sharps, follow this rule:
Go **up a half step** from the **last sharp** in the key signature.
The name of that note is the name of the key.

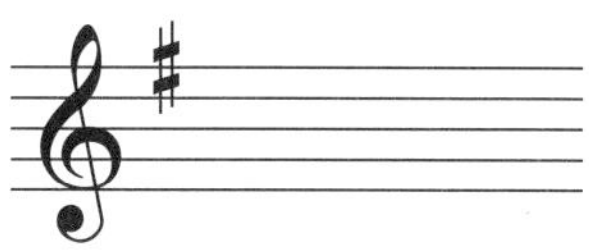

Ex. Last sharp: F#
Key name: G

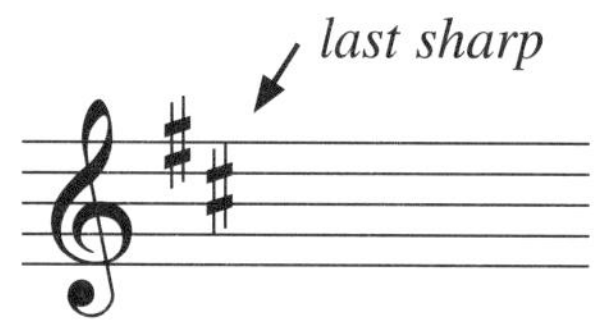

Ex. Last sharp: C#
Key name: D

Last sharp: ____
Key name: ____
(you write)

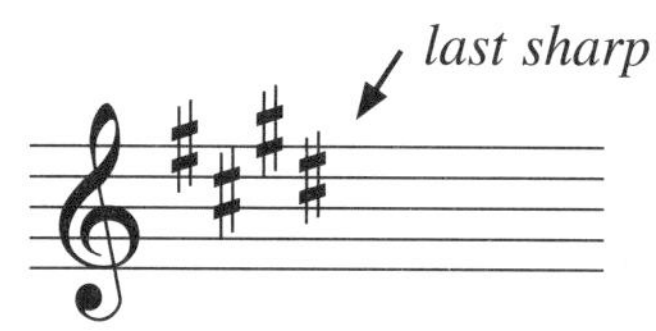

Last sharp: ____
Key name: ____
(you write)

Hint: The last sharp in the key signature is the **leading tone** of the key.

The Sharp Pattern

1. The pattern of sharps is always the same. Study the example and the rules below.

- First, always begin with **F♯** for both clefs.
- Continue the pattern moving **down a 4th** and **up a 5th**.
- After the fourth sharp, **D♯**, move down to **A♯**. Then continue the "up 5, down 4" pattern.

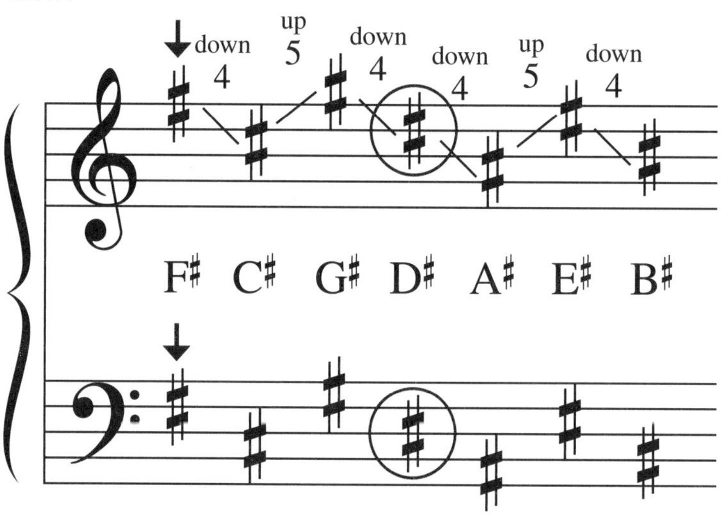

2. **Sharp Pattern Tip:** This silly sentence may help you remember the sharp pattern.

<u>F</u>at <u>C</u>ats <u>G</u>o <u>D</u>own <u>A</u>lleys <u>E</u>ating <u>B</u>ugs

3. Write the complete **sharp pattern** six times in the treble and bass clefs.
Refer to the example and rules on p. 104.

(you write)

(you write)

(you write)

(you write)

(you write)

(you write)

2-Octave Scales: D, A, and E Major

- Notice each scale is played **forte**, then **piano**. Listen for steady rhythm with an even tone.

LEARNING VIDEO

D Major Scale

LEARNING VIDEO

A MAJOR Scale

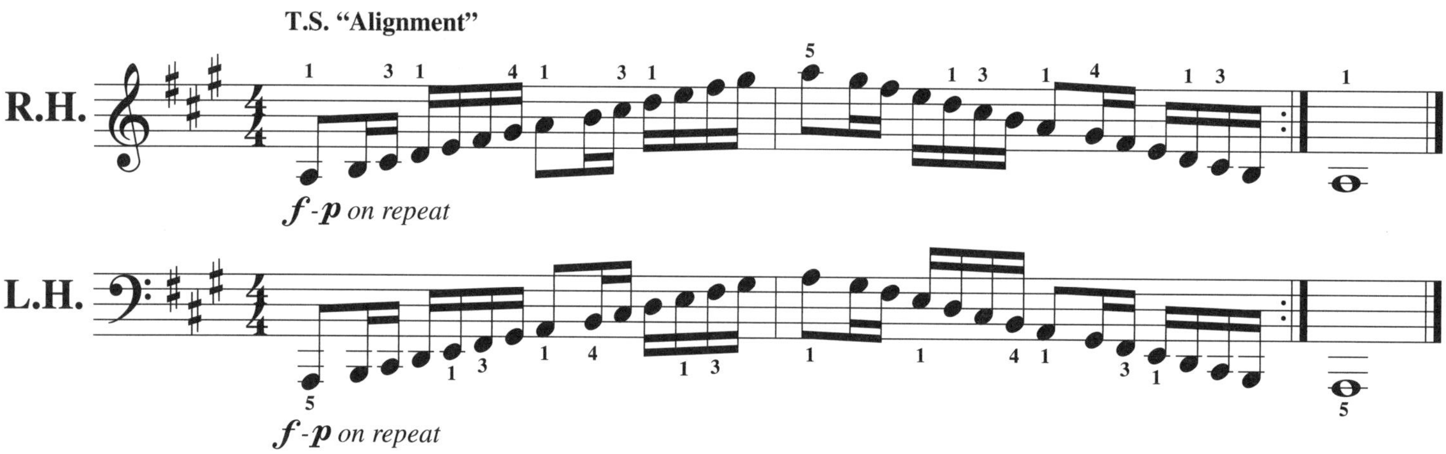

LEARNING VIDEO

E Major Scale

Optional: ____ ♩ = 72 *Andante* ____ ♩ = 100 *Moderato* ____ ♩ = 112 *Allegro*

TECHNIQUE SECRET 4
Half Circle/Full Circle, p.15

LEARNING VIDEO

D Major Primary Chords

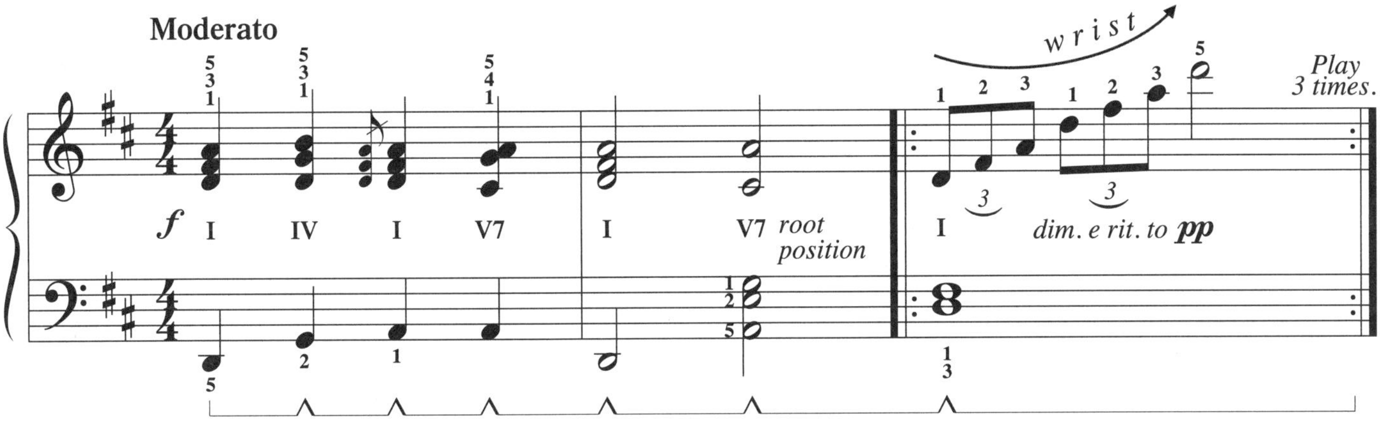

LEARNING VIDEO

A MAJOR Primary Chords

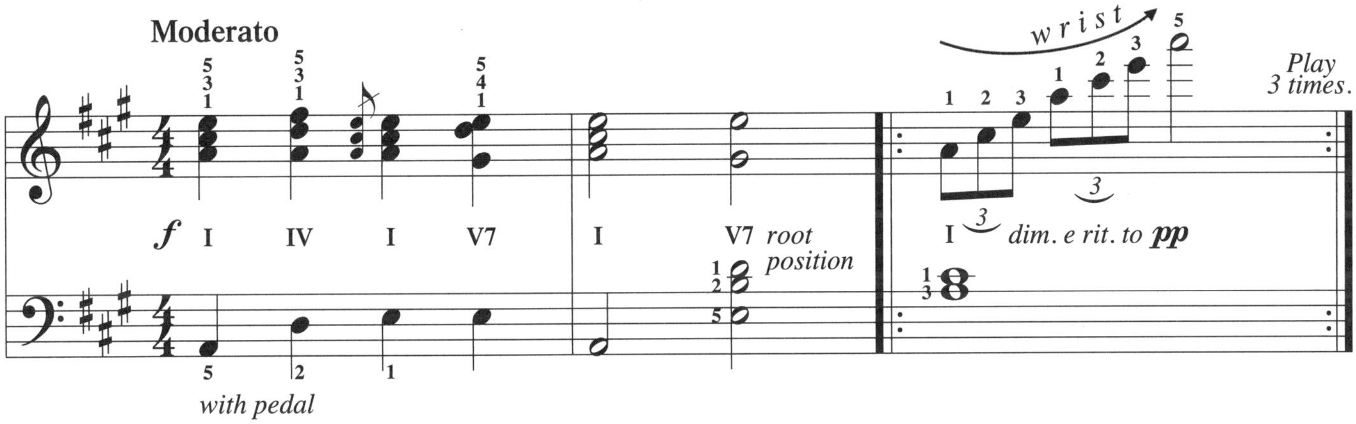

LEARNING VIDEO

E Major Primary Chords

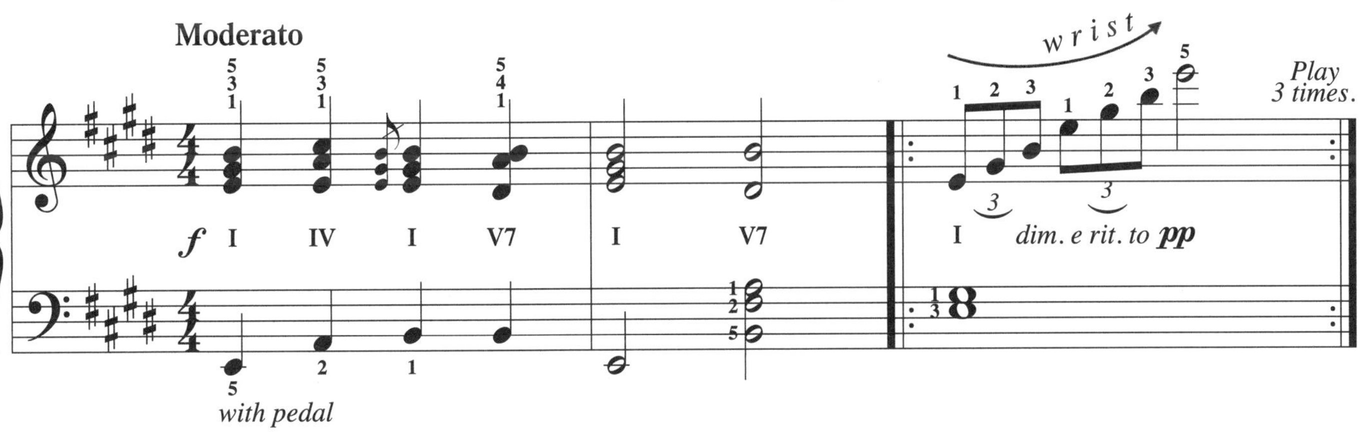

Review: An **accidental** is a sharp, flat or natural that is not in the key signature.

Rhythm Hint: Set a strong, **internal steady beat** for the opening half notes. This will establish the pace for the entire piece.

LEARNING VIDEO

Ceremony for Peace

Key of ____Major

Moderately, majestically

N. Faber

DISCOVERY

Find two measures where the right hand plays a **G major chord** and its inversions.

Key of D: Playing a Lead Sheet

THEORY

A **lead sheet** consists of a melody with **chord symbols** shown above the staff. The chord symbols indicate the harmony to be played with your left hand.

Directions for The Blue Danube:

1. Play the melody alone (page 111).
2. Next, play the **Blocked Chord Warm-up** below.
3. Then, play the melody with **blocked chords** on beat 1 of each measure. Follow the chord symbols!

D Major Blocked Chord Warm-up

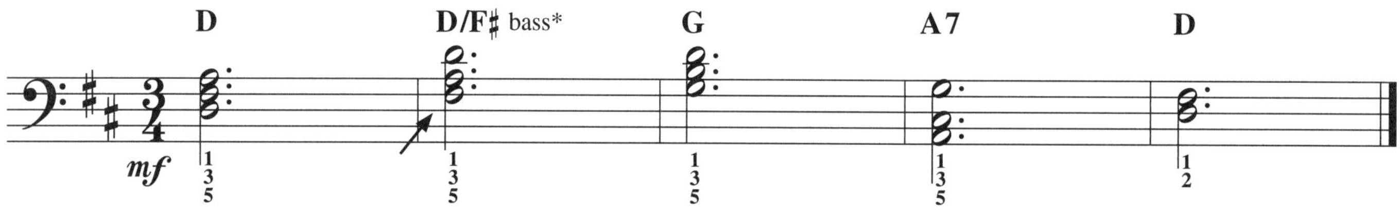

*The letter after a slash mark indicates the **bass note** of a chord inversion.

4. Practice this **Broken Chord Warm-up**.
5. Lastly, play the melody slowly with this **L.H.** accompaniment. See the example below.

D Major Broken Chord Warm-up

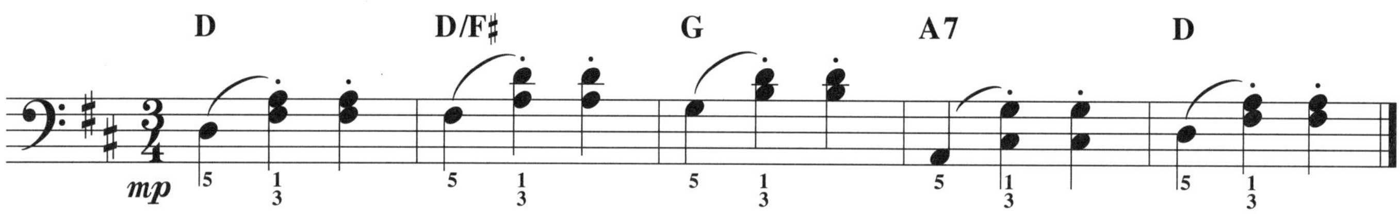

Example:

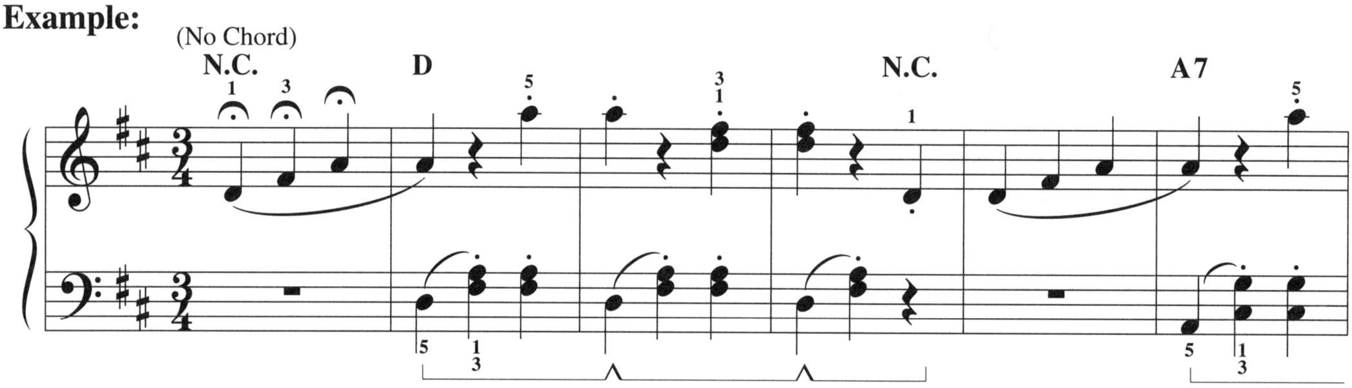

Adventure Quote | *"Melody is the essence of music." –Mozart*

Lead Sheet for

The Blue Danube*

Key of ___ Major

LEARNING VIDEO

Johann Strauss II
(1825-1899, Austria)

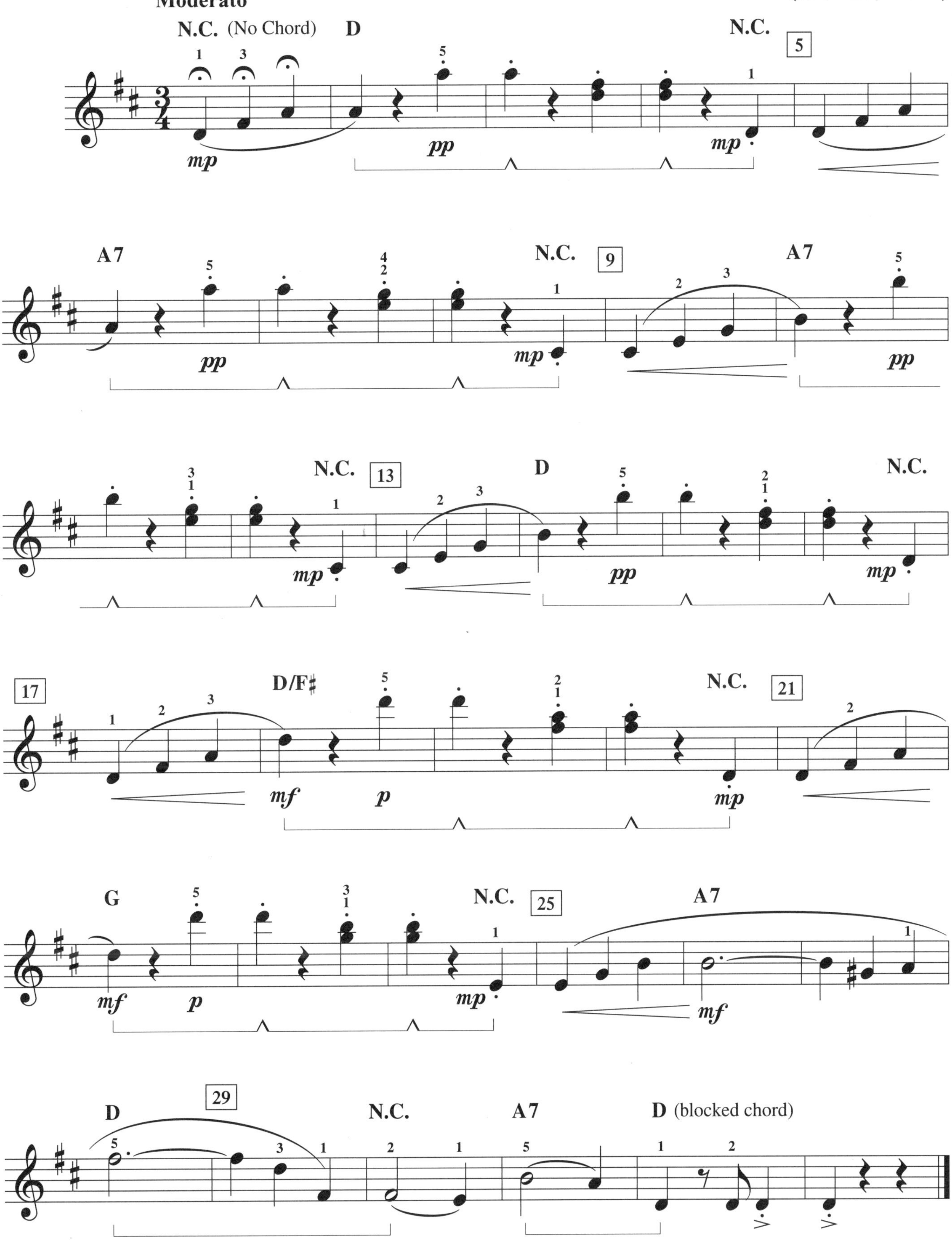

*The Danube River is the second largest river in Europe.

Writing in the "Land of D Major"

THEORY

1. "Map out" the territory for **D major**.

- Write the key signature for each clef.
- Write a **one-octave D major scale** ascending and descending. Use whole notes.
- Shade in the sharped notes. Label the *tonic* (**T**), *dominant* (**D**), and *leading tone* (**LT**).

2. Circle **root position**, **1st inversion**, or **2nd inversion** for each example.

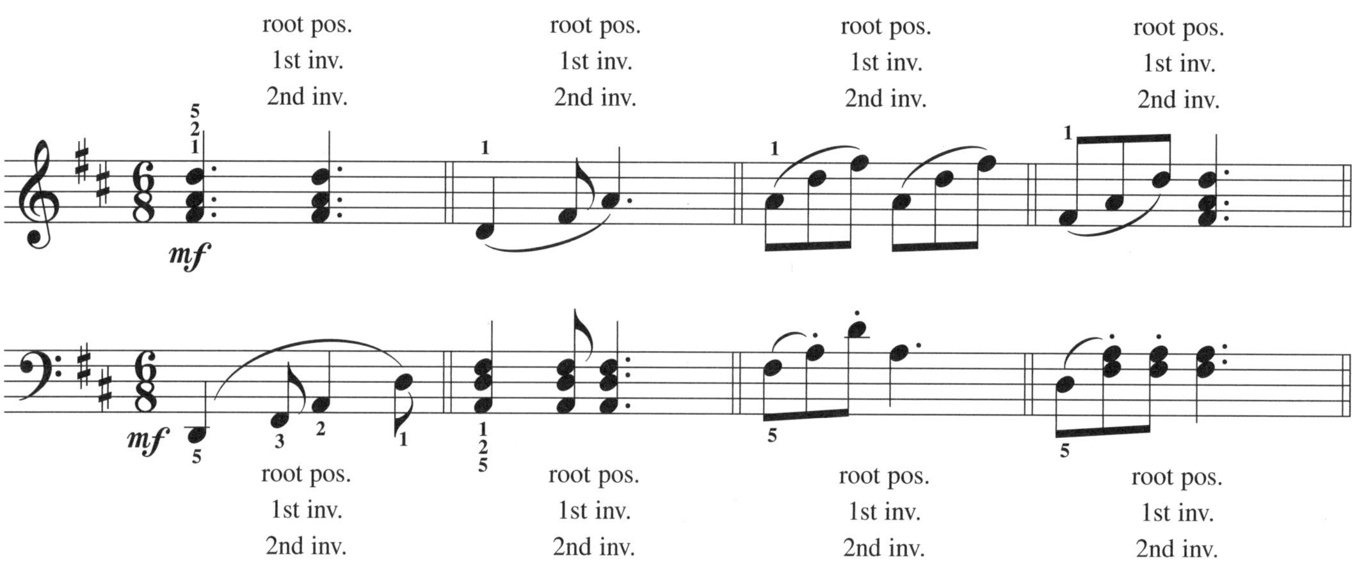

3. Complete the **Question** and **Answer** melody. Remember, the Question ends on any note *except* the tonic. The Answer *always* ends on the tonic.

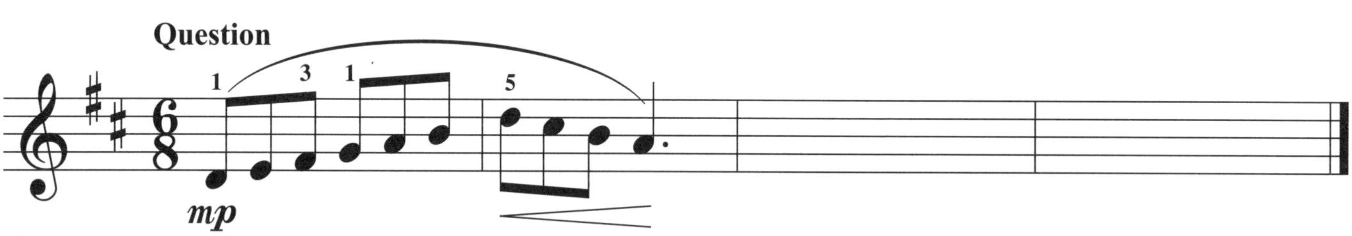

4. Add slurs, dynamics, and fingering for your Answer. Play and enjoy the completed melody.

The Leading Tone Leads the Way

To find the name of the sharp key signature:

- Find the last sharp—the one farthest to the right.
  This is the leading tone.
- Now go up a **half step** to the tonic—the name of the key.

1. Name each key signature.

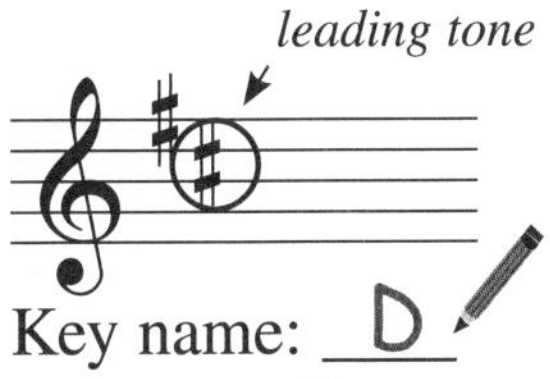

Key name: D
Ex.

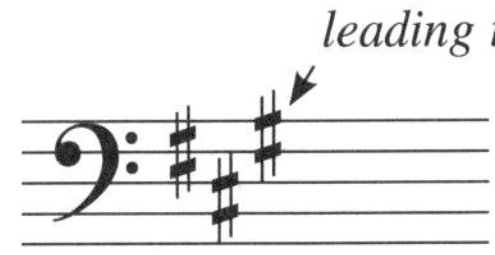

Key name: ____

Key name: ____

Key name: ____

Key name: ____

Key name: ____

Key name: ____

Key name: ____

Key name: ____

Key name: ____

(Notice these key names will include a sharp.)

Key name: ____ ♯

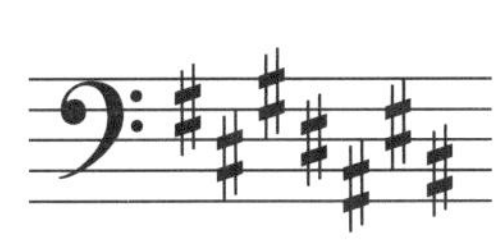

Key name: ____ ♯

Review: The Order of Sharps

2. Remember, the order of the **7 sharps** is always the same: **F♯ C♯ G♯ D♯ A♯ E♯ B♯**.
Here's another silly sentence that may help:

Funny **C**ats **G**reet **D**ogs **A**nd **E**ducate **B**ears

You may also enjoy creating a sentence yourself:

____

Molto means "very."
For example, *molto rit.* means
to make a very big *ritardando*.
See measure 30.

LEARNING VIDEO

Wild Flowers

Key of ___ Major

Moderato, espressivo

N. Faber

Adventure Quote | "Slow and steady wins the race." -Aesop's Fable

LEARNING VIDEO

• Combining the **staccato L.H. octaves** with **pedal** produces a celebratory sound!

Spring*

Key of ___ Major

Antonio Vivaldi
(1678-1741, Italy)
arranged

*from "The Four Seasons"

Adventure Quote | *"The four seasons are the four parts of the year, but they are also the four parts of life."*
-Antonio Vivaldi

20
mp
22
f
24
26
p
29
molto rit.
mf

Review these time signatures.

3/8	=	**3 beats in one measure** **♪ gets 1 beat**	**6/8** =	**6 beats in one measure** **♪ gets 1 beat**

1. • Write **1 2 3** under the **correct beats** for this melody.
• Then sightread at a rather slow tempo, while counting aloud, "1 2 3."

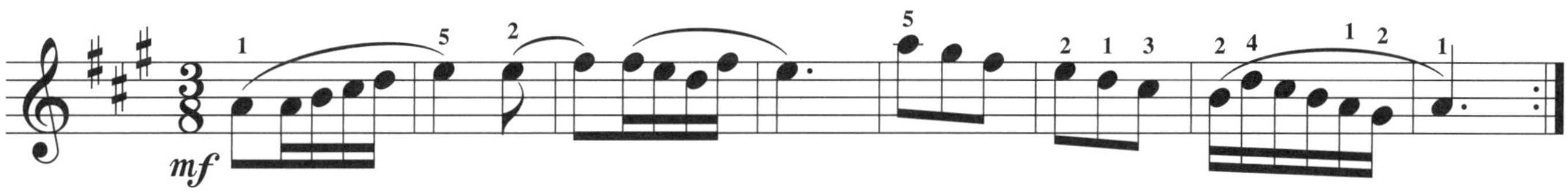

2. • Write **1 2 3 4 5 6** under the **correct beats** for this melody.
• Then sightread at a very slow tempo, while counting aloud, "1 2 3 4 5 6."

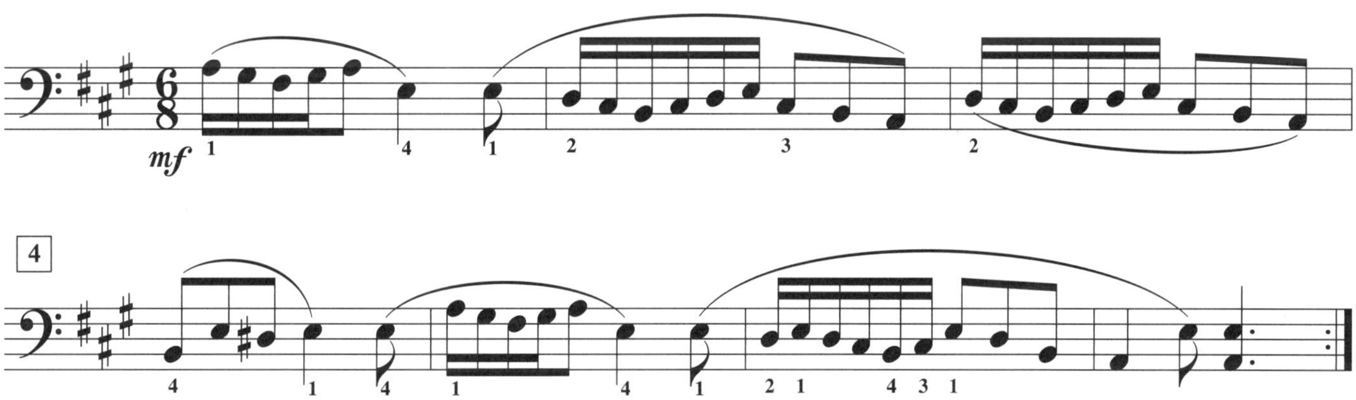

3. Write **4 measures** of your own rhythm in 6/8 time. Use **16th notes** in every measure.

Here are some common patterns: 

Gigue – (pronounced "zheeg") is a lively Baroque dance.

LEARNING VIDEO

In old English theater, the performance of a play would often conclude with a **gigue** and dancing.

Gigue in A Major

DISCOVERY Does the **B** section begin on the *tonic* or *dominant?*

TECHNIQUE

- Use the **"half circle/full circle"** wrist motion for the arpeggios. Notice the arrows in measures 1 and 17.

LEARNING VIDEO

Summer Solstice

Key of ___ Major

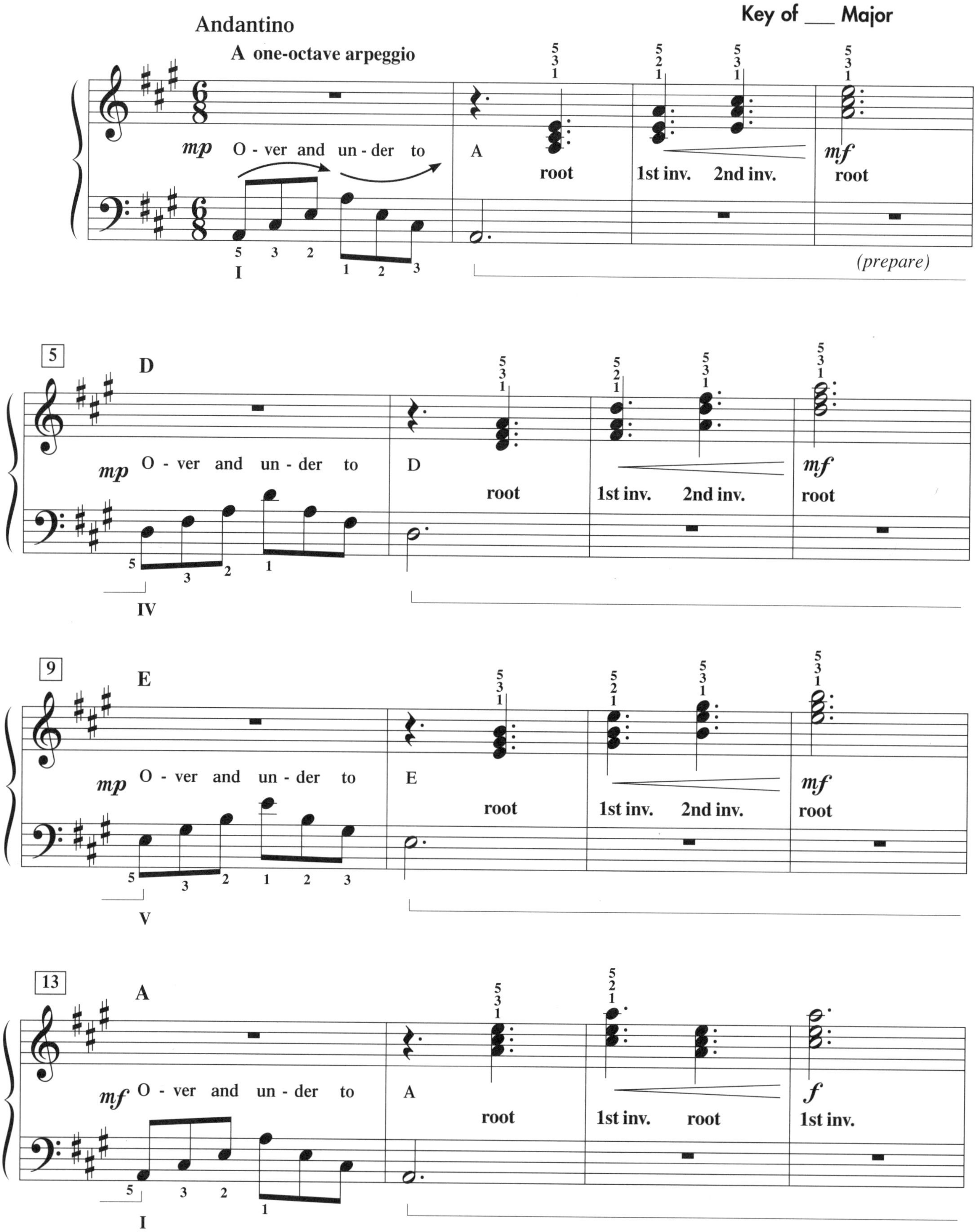

DISCOVERY Name the chords for *measures 17-34*.
Write the **letter names** above the staff and the **Roman numerals** below.

Writing in the "Land of A Major"

THEORY

1. "Map out" the territory for **A major.**

- Write the key signature for each clef.
- Write a **one-octave A major scale** ascending and descending. Use whole notes.
- Shade in the sharped notes. Label the *tonic* (**T**), *dominant* (**D**), and *leading tone* (**LT**).

key signature

R.H.

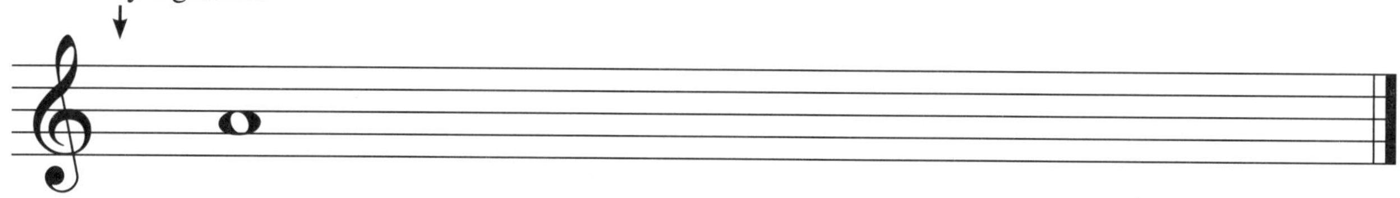

key signature

L.H.

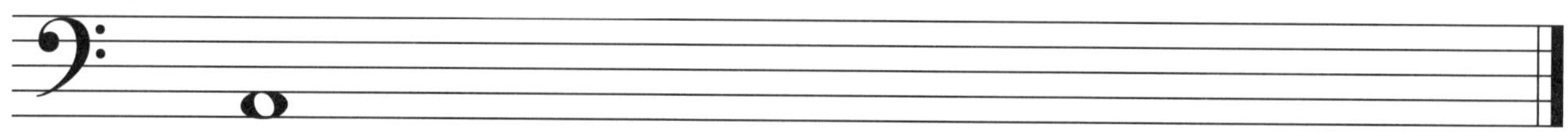

2. Circle **root position**, **1st inversion**, or **2nd inversion** for each example.

root pos.	root pos.	root pos.	root pos.
1st inv.	1st inv.	1st inv.	1st inv.
2nd inv.	2nd inv.	2nd inv.	2nd inv.

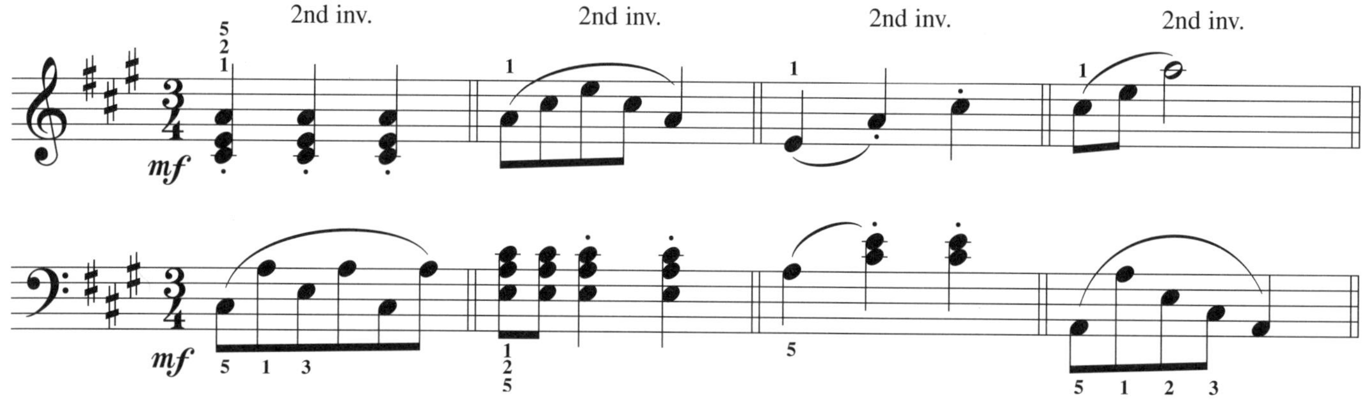

root pos.	root pos.	root pos.	root pos.
1st inv.	1st inv.	1st inv.	1st inv.
2nd inv.	2nd inv.	2nd inv.	2nd inv.

3. Complete the **Question** and **Answer** melody. Add slurs, dynamics, and fingering.
Play and enjoy!

1. • First, learn this **D major accompaniment**. Play while your teacher *improvises* a **melody** higher using notes from the **D major scale**.

• Reverse! You **improvise** while your teacher plays the duet. Hint: Try beginning using only the sharped keys, **F♯** and **C♯**!

D improv
Spring Rain

LEARNING VIDEO

2. • Now learn this **A major accompaniment**. Play while your teacher *improvises* a **melody** higher using notes from the **A major scale**.

• Reverse! You **improvise** while your teacher plays the duet.

LEARNING VIDEO

A improv rustling wind

Poco a poco means "little by little."
cresc. poco a poco means to
get louder little by little.

LEARNING VIDEO

Great Barrier Reef

Key of ___ Major

- Begin quietly and build gradually to a stately, majestic sound.

Stately (♩ = 88-96)

N. Faber

The world's largest reef system (reefs and islands) is the Great Barrier Reef, off the coast of northeast Australia. The amazing reef structure was built by billions of tiny organisms and can actually be seen from outer space. It has been called one of the seven natural wonders of the world.

DISCOVERY

Does the *opening* chord have the root, 3rd, or 5th on top (as the melody)? _____
Does the *final* chord have the root, 3rd, or 5th on top? _____

Keyboard Pattern for Sharp Keys

THEORY

1. Play and memorize this **sharp pattern**. Say the words aloud.
This pattern is a quick "keyboard trick" for remembering the sharp keys!

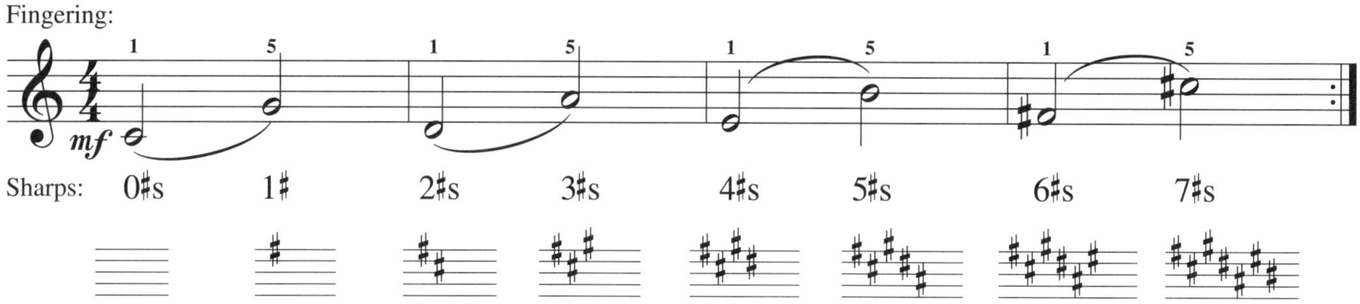

2. Close the keyboard. Can you play the pattern in your mind's eye?
Now use the pattern to help you write the key signatures below.

Key of D major

Ex. 2 sharps

Key of G major

____ sharp

Key of A major

____ sharps

Key of A major

____ sharps

Key of E major

____ sharps

Key of D major

____ sharps

Key of B major

____ sharps

Key of E major

____ sharps

Key of F♯ major

____ sharps

Key of B major

____ sharps

Key of G major

____ sharp

Key of C♯ major

____ sharps

- Name each key signature.
- Then write the interval up or down.

Key of ____ major

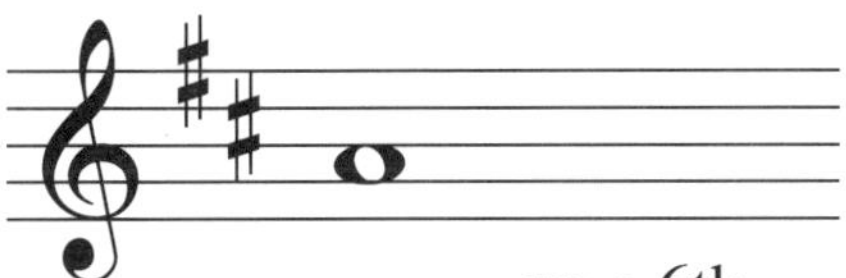

up a 6th

Key of ____ major

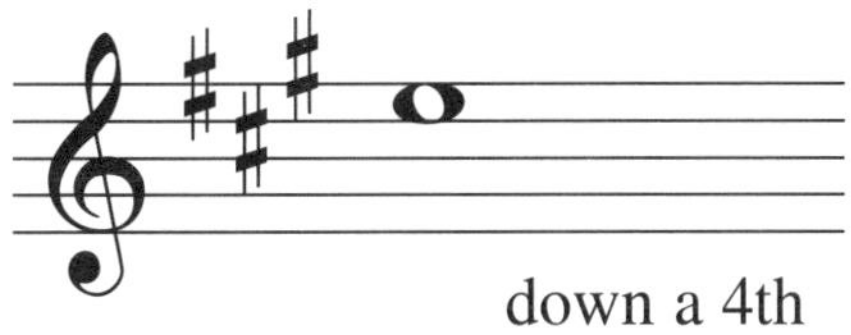

down a 4th

Key of ____ major

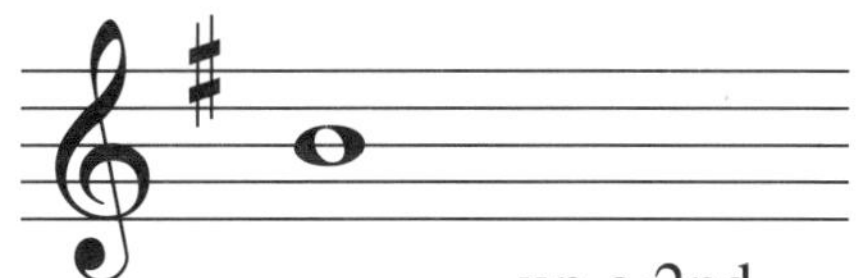

up a 2nd

Key of ____ major

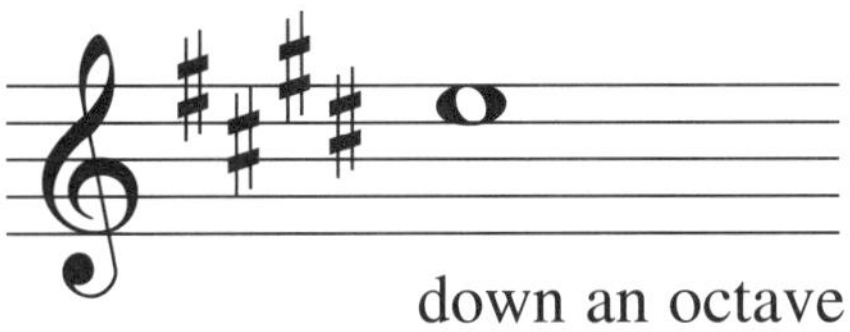

down an octave

Key of ____ major

up a 3rd

Key of ____ major

down a 5th

Key of ____ major

up a 5th

Key of ____ major

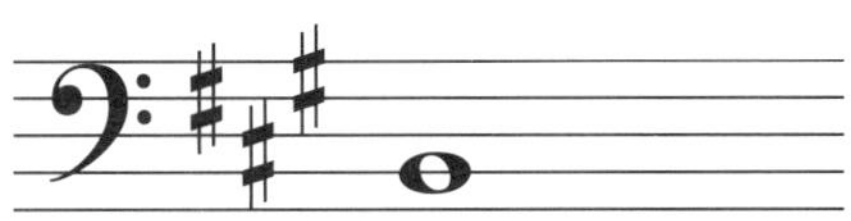

up a 7th

Key of ____ major

down a 6th

Ear-Training Playback

- Close your eyes (or face away from the keyboard).
- Your teacher will name the key and play a short melody that begins on the *tonic.*
- Listen carefully as it is played twice. Then play back the melody at the piano.

For Teacher Use Only: (The examples below may be played in any order and repeated several times.)
Note: Play rather slowly.

Say: "Key of D major"

Say: "Key of A major"

Say: "Key of G major"

Say: "Key of D major"

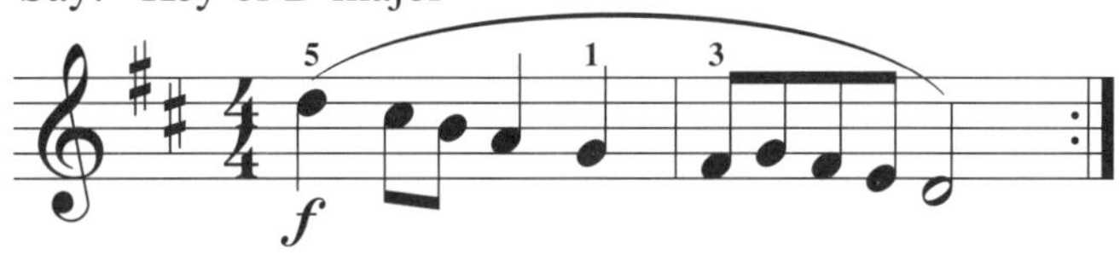

LEARNING VIDEO

These three blues pieces portray music of the 1920's in three American cities.

Review: If the tempo marking suggests *swing*, play the eighth notes in a **long-short** rhythm pattern.

Three Blues Pieces for Piano

1. New Orleans, 1928

Slow swing (♩ = 80-92)

Key of ___ Major

N. Faber

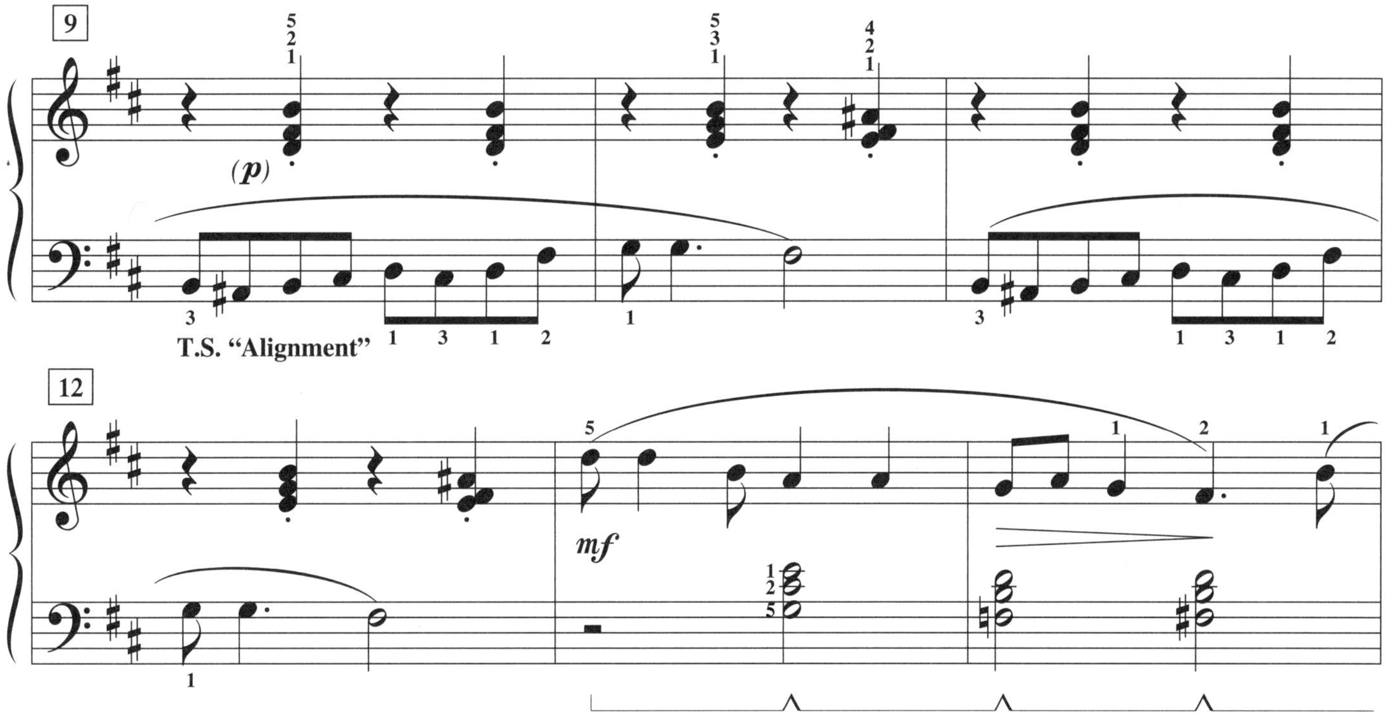

Dal Segno al Coda: "from the sign to the coda."
Return to the 𝄋 sign and play to 𝄌,
then jump to the Coda (ending).

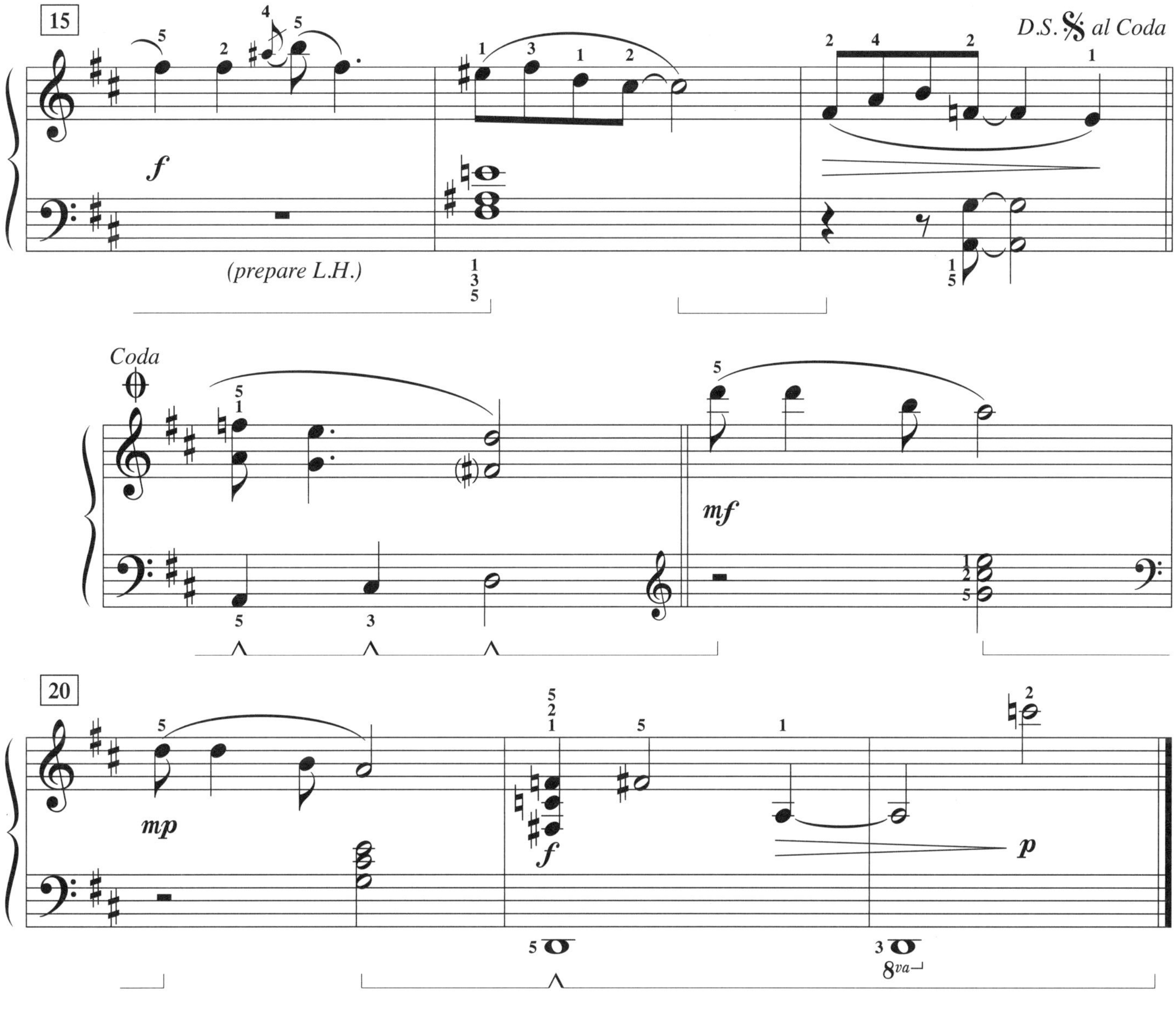

Fast Stomp in Swing in a Sharp Key

A **"stomp"** is a type of jazz tune popular in early jazz with a fast tempo and a driving rhythmic beat.

LEARNING VIDEO

2. Kansas City, 1928

Key of ___ Major

Moderately fast swing (♩ = 144-160)

Adventure Quote | *"Rhythm is the amazing use of time—propelling the music forward, or holding it back—but always vital and the essence of it all."* –Anonymous

DISCOVERY

Name the scale used in *measures 17* and *18.*

Jazz music has many moods, tempos, keys, chords, and rhythms. Its possibilities are endless! This piece in E major has a broad, sophisticated sound with a **bluesy, "big city" character.**

LEARNING VIDEO

3. Manhattan, 1928

Key of ___ Major

Adventure Quote | *"A piano is not just a collection of keys; it is a symphony of possibilities waiting to be explored." -Anonymous*

26
L.H.
L.H. 2/4 over
R.H. 4
29
L.H. 2/4 over
R.H. 3
33
mp
mf
36
ff
molto rit.
39
Slowly
R.H.
L.H. over
L.H.
sfz
8va

Hint: Use **rotation*** in *measure 3* for each exercise.

- Practice at slow, medium, and fast tempi.
- Play these exercises by memory.

LEARNING VIDEO

Awesome A Major

LEARNING VIDEO

Electrifying E Major

Rotation is a gentle side-to-side rocking motion of the hand—rather like turning a key in a lock. (Level 3A Technique Secret 3)

Writing in the "Land of E Major"

THEORY

1. "Map out" the territory for **E major**.

- Write the key signature for each clef.
- Write a **one-octave E major scale** ascending and descending. Use whole notes.
- Shade in the sharped notes. Label the *tonic* (**T**), *dominant* (**D**), and *leading tone* (**LT**).

key signature

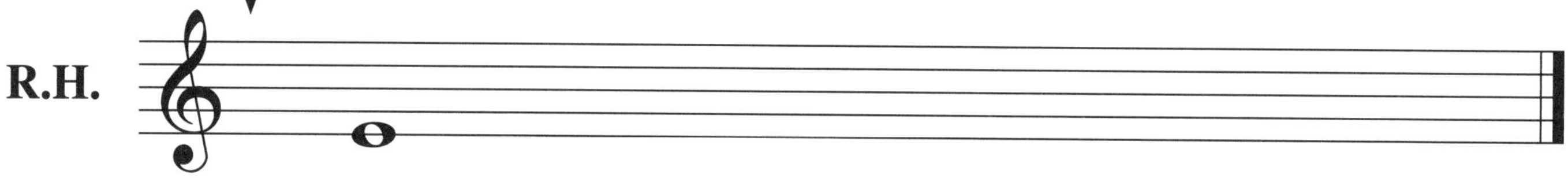

key signature

2. Circle **root position**, **1st inversion**, or **2nd inversion** for each example.

root pos. 1st inv. 2nd inv.	root pos. 1st inv. 2nd inv.	root pos. 1st inv. 2nd inv.	root pos. 1st inv. 2nd inv.

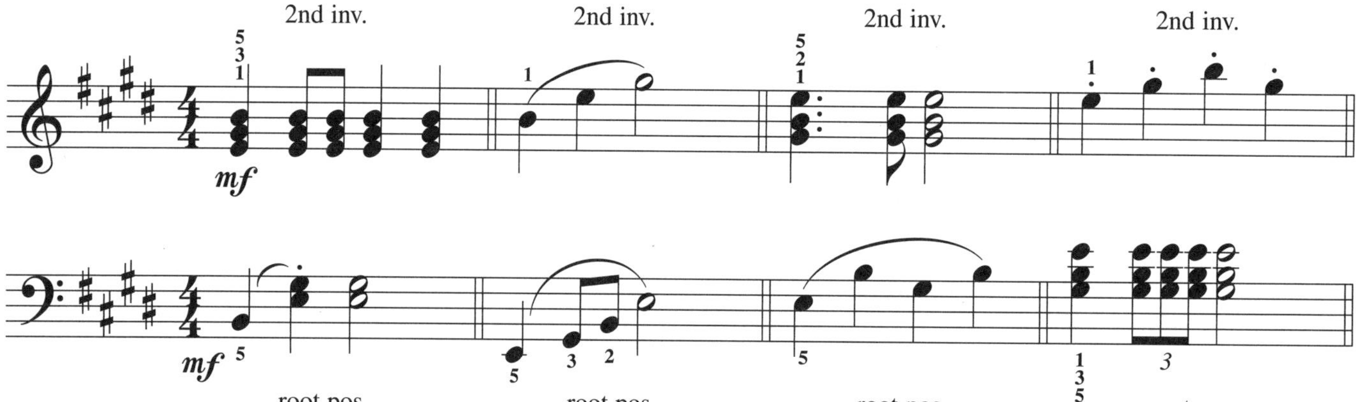

root pos. 1st inv. 2nd inv.	root pos. 1st inv. 2nd inv.	root pos. 1st inv. 2nd inv.	root pos. 1st inv. 2nd inv.

3. Complete the **Question** and **Answer** melody. Add slurs, dynamics, and fingering.
Play and enjoy!

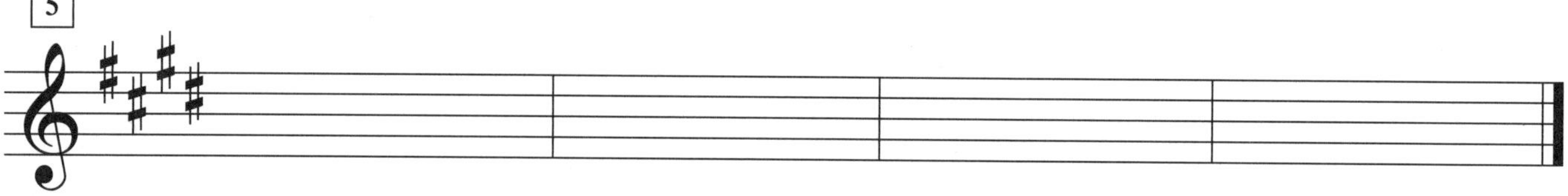

EYE TRAINING

Chant the **scale steps** to help you learn this song. Can you play it by memory?

LEARNING VIDEO

Scale-Step Waltz in E Major

Transpose to other sharp keys: **G**, **D**, and **A**.

EAR TRAINING

Close your eyes and listen to your teacher play an example.
On what scale step does it end—1, 2, 3, 4, 5, 6, or 7? Tell your teacher.

For Teacher Use Only: (The examples below may be played in any order and repeated several times.)

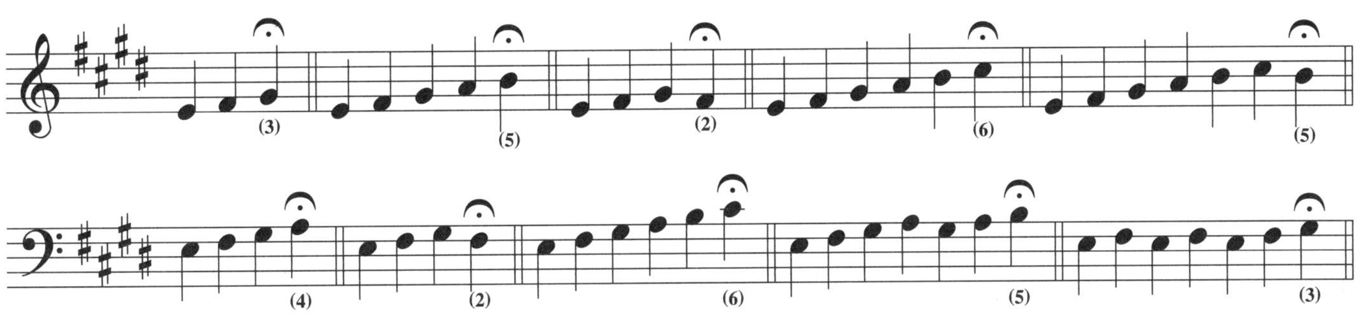

This prelude is one of **Johann Sebastian Bach's** most famous keyboard pieces. Remember, a small musical idea is called a **motive**. Bach was a master at creating an entire composition from a **single musical idea** or motive.

Bach's original manuscript did not include dynamic marks. The dynamic marks given here show one **interpretation** for the piece. Explore your own dynamic marks and articulations.

Congratulations on being able to play this famous piece from the **keyboard repertoire!**

Prelude in C*

Andante

Johann Sebastian Bach
(1685-1750, Germany)
original form

*No. 1 from *The Well-Tempered Clavier*, Book 1

7
9
11
cresc.
13
mf
dim.
15
p

17
mp
19
p
21
mp
cresc.
23
mf
25
cresc.

Where does the L.H. bass note stay in the *dominant* for 8 consecutive measures?

Certificate of Completion

CONGRATULATIONS TO

____

(Your name)

You have completed PIANO ADVENTURES®

The GRAND Level 4!

Teacher: ____________________________

Date: ____________________________

You are now ready for the LEVEL 4 Theory and Performance Exams. Visit exams.pianoadventures.com

Then what awaits?

Level 5!

More marvelous music.